THE WONDER OF IMPROVISATION

AL WUNDER

WP

This book is dedicated to

My father whose advice on happiness was, "Do
what you like doing, just make sure you do it well".

and to

My mentor, Alwin Nikolais, whose genius, warmth and
inspiration helped me to discover and develop
what I truly love doing, improvisation.

First published by Wunder Publishers 2006
64 Ascot Hall Road, Ascot Victoria 3364
Second printing   December 2009
alwunder@theatreoftheordinary.com

ISBN   0-646-455559

Printer	High Tech Printing Ballarat
Cover Design	Tina Libertone
Book layout	Al Wunder
Editors	Patricia Sykes and Lynden Nicholls
Proof readers	Chris Hinton, Francis Nicholls-Wunder, James Cunnigham

Acknowledgments

I am a firm believer in the chaos theory and offer thanks to the butterfly in China whose beating wings somehow led to me writing "The Wonder of Improvisation". There are, of course, several people who had a more direct influence on my life, my teaching and the completion of this book.

I will be eternally grateful to my mentor, Alwin Nikolais, his genius as a teacher and choreographer of modern dance totally changed my life and put me on the path I travel today.

Fate brought Terry Sendgraff and Ruth Zaporah into my life the first year I started teaching on my own. At first they were my students, then colleagues, then my teachers. Without their influence I might still be doing a newspaper route in Berkeley, California. Terry, with her constant expressions of love for me and faith in my teaching, remains to this day the most influential person in my life.

It is with immense pleasure that I thank the many, many students, professionals and non-professionals alike who have taught me so much about my own teaching. It was the smiles, the beauty and the poignant tears they brought to the classroom that told me I was doing something right and helped me to understand where to take my next step.

To my wife, Lynden Nicholls, I give three kisses for taking photographs, co-editing this book, and spending many hours discussing with me my teaching methods and philosophy. Her discerning eye and ear has been an invaluable help.

There is a box of old and new photographs on top of a filing cabinet next to my desk. Some of those photos appear in this book. To George Kyriacou, Phil Makana, Rosemary Simons, Lynden Nicholls and several unknown photographers whose names did not grace the back of their work I offer heartfelt thanks.

Technology also gets a handshake as my trusty old Panasonic and brand new Sony camcorders combined with my NEC dvd recorder to produce many of the images. The computer age with its world wide web allowed me to reconnect with Murray Louis, Gladys Bailin and Phyllis Lamhut, my first teachers, who graciously sent via the internet photos of themselves.

I am grateful for insights offered by James McCaughey, John Jenkins and my son Francis Nicholls-Wunder through the various stages my writing took me. A special thanks to Adrienne Liebman whose not so gentle Jewish motherly prodding to write about my work eventually got me doing it.

Finally there is Trish Sykes. Without her this book would not exist. Trish began a journey with me in 1998. She was my student of improvisation who became my writing mentor. We spent six years in this wonderful symbiotic relationship as she guided me through the long process of putting pen to paper, fingers to computer keyboard and finally how to put improvised meandering thoughts into well-constructed sentences. I will forever cherish the hours we spent together and her enduring patience, encouragement and friendship.

Contents

Foreword
By Andrew Morrish

...the gentle subversive

I first met Al on his arrival in Australia in July 1982, and, with typical antipodean mistrust of all things American, expected to meet a ruthless, self promoting, ego maniac. I was surprised by his shy gentleness, and also that Wunder is indeed his real name.

The other experience was of instant comfort in his classes. At last I had found work in dance and movement that did not consist of hard things to do that hurt when you tried. I felt physically accepted, rather than shaped, and aesthetically satisfied. I had no understanding of how or why this was the case, but knew that I had found my first artistic home in his approach.

Twenty years later, I have witnessed thousands of people have this experience, and come to understand the mechanics of Al's approach and how it facilitates the development of a personal performance style. Of great significance is the congruence between what it is that Al teaches and the values with which he teaches. This book will talk as much about these values as it does about the "how to's". It is also a piece of living history, explaining the influences and circumstances that have brought about his extraordinary contribution to improvisation performance practice.

In his twenty year career in Australia, I have only heard him say "don't do that" to a student once. Yes it was me! I had been repeating a particularly annoying sound-something between a groan and a whistle-for some minutes, during the preparation of the performance at the end of his initial visit. I am pretty sure that the particular sound also had a disturbing effect on his hearing aids.

However, the point is that Al's process does not consist of a series of shapings of the student ie "don't do this, do that" type teaching. He asks the student to detail what it was that they enjoyed in what they did. Through this, their experience of performing becomes embedded in their experiences of satisfaction and interest. A personal style evolves in this process.

His accepting position is often questioned by more conventional theatre practitioners. "How can improvement occur without critique?" they ask.

Al's position reflects two things. One is his deep belief in developmental forces that produce growth, when support is provided, and the second is that it is more important that the performer is empowered in this path, rather than holding the teacher (even appreciatively) responsible.

A further example of this became apparent the first time that I performed in a shared programme with other dance practitioners after working with Al for 3 years. I was shocked by their levels of anxiety prior to performing, marked by little practices of the material in an irritatingly crowded dressing room. Equally shocking to me was the intense debate that followed their performance, with much focus on the mistakes they had made. The contrast to the ethos that Al had created in my own practice was striking.

One of the most useful aspects of improvisational training is its emphasis on the decisions of the performer, and the inherent encouragement to take responsibility for them. In this sense, Al's work maintains the initial subversive intent of contemporary improvisation practice which began in the late 60's and early 70's in the United States. Without being ideological, the day to day pragmatic of Al's training process undermines many of the constructs that are implicit in some other forms of contemporary performance practice. He encourages the development of a personal 'outside eye" in performance, and this in combination with the empowerment of a personal aesthetic holds out the carrot of "new form" to the intrepid. His work genuinely seeks to work outside the conventions of theatrical form, where rules of "good performance" are tacitly held. It is a gentle undoing that endorses a wide range of performance states, intensities, styles and intentions. It eschews the development of a generic style. Al is the gentle subversive who achieves his aim by the consistent application of profound humanistic constructs.

25

The Improvisational work of Al Wunder has been a tremendous influence on many performers in Australia and this book is long overdue. It will help others to perform improvisationally and sets out an ethos for how teaching might occur. I can only say that I am delighted that Al has finished it, and daily grateful for both his work and its ethos.

Andrew Morrish

Al Wunder   Andrew Morrish

INTRODUCTION
"I have planned nothing and that has kept me very busy."[1]

When I was fourteen years old a woman said to me, "With a name like yours you should be in show business". My name has always provoked witty comments; Are you really A. Wunder? Will Wunders never cease? Or when a certain singer became famous; are you related to Stevie? Connecting my name to a career in show business was something new and quite interesting at that time in my life even though I loved singing and dancing. The facts that I sang off tune and danced with a pronounced limp made the prospect of actually involving myself in the performing arts seem quite remote. A genetic hearing loss and a few accidental happenings had conspired to limit my potential of becoming a Broadway star. In fact I had never even contemplated becoming a performer and was quite content with leading an ordinary life.

But no one leads an ordinary life. No one! We are all special; our lives filled with a range of experiences that take us from birth to death, each of us unique because of the circumstances that shape who we are. There are his stories, her stories, our stories, their stories, your story and my story, each one interesting in its own right. The chance happenings that we encounter and life-defining choices that we make in our personal journeys can be of immense interest to friends we meet along the way. The fact that someone might be famous does not make her life history any more important than the average Jane or Joe living quietly on the street where you live. I have such a strong belief that everyone's story is worth telling that I call what I teach *Theatre of the Ordinary*. Yes, the aforementioned woman was prophetic in linking my surname to a profession in the performing arts. I didn't make it on Broadway or in the movies, but developed with the help of a few friends, a not so ordinary form of theatre.

---

[1] A statement on a flier Ruth Zaporah used for one of her performance series.

The most unique aspect of Theatre of the Ordinary is, as its name suggests, a theatre where ordinary non-professional performers can regularly put themselves on stage and perform in front of an appreciative audience. What continues to surprise and delight me is the number of talented professionals in dance, theatre and music who also attend classes and perform alongside computer programmers, social workers, visual artists, maths teachers, house painters, electricians, part-time workers and unemployed people.

Another element that distinguishes the performances of Theatre of the Ordinary from most other forms of theatre is the fact that they are totally improvised utilising movement, text, sound and or song to communicate to an audience. There are no pre-planned ideas or suggestions of character traits given by the audience, just the performer or performers alone in the space with developed skills, past experiences and confidence in their ability to create something from nothing. Performers are not just performers. They are also the writers, composers, choreographers and directors of their own performance pieces. The first sounds, words or movements become the genesis for a theatrical event that has not been rehearsed and will never be seen again.

This is quite unusual. Improvised performances are often structured to varying degrees. The very popular Theatre Sports uses a competition based set up where two teams of actors are given specific scenarios to improvise within. Contact Improvisation, a dance form that has become extremely popular in many countries around the world, has, as its structure, the use of the physical contact between two dancers as a pivot point from which beautiful and exciting lifts and rotations are created. Jazz musicians tend to combine composed sections with several solos using the melody line and chord progressions to improvise around.

The attraction of all different types of people to Theatre of the Ordinary classes still remains a bit of a mystery to me. I believe that a person will have several reasons, some conscious and some they aren't aware of yet, that inspire them to continue developing as improvising performers. Using my own feelings as a guide I would suggest that the combination of playfulness, emotional risk taking, intellectual challenge and physical expansiveness all play their part in keeping students coming back for more. Deep in my heart I believe, simply because it has been so valuable for me, that the most attractive element of improvised performance is the spontaneous communication that happens between audience and performer.

When performing, a situation is set up where those onstage have a metaphorical dialogue with the audience. All movements and speaking are intended to communicate to the audience. This communication to a large group of people creates a need to engage in conversation that is more meaningful, insightful and entertaining than if we were talking to a few friends in a coffee shop. Because of its improvised nature the message being stated will be an observation of what is happening in our lives at that moment even if it is a purely physical dance piece without a single word spoken.

For most of us performing can be quite frightening. The fear that we won't measure up, won't be as good as... keeps us from putting ourselves in the spotlight. Improvising can be scarier since we cannot develop and rehearse what we are going to do. I believe however that it is this fear of being boring or inadequate that inspires us to be more eloquent, simply because we feel we have to be good when communicating to an audience. Once that fear is alleviated and the confidence of doing a solo in front of spectators grows, the telling of our stories in a theatrical way becomes richer. The flow between light-hearted and more serious material becomes easier. Skills developed in the expressive use of movement, words and sounds emerge more effortlessly.

This is what "Theatre of the Ordinary" is all about. It is a showing of ourselves rather than a showing off of what we can do. It creates a non-competitive performance space for anyone to theatrically present their story of the day to an audience of friends, colleagues and strangers.

The "Wonder of Improvisation" is a book about me. It is a written performance about my story, the influences that led me to where I am today, the people I met who guided and helped me develop my philosophy of teaching and the methodology I use to teach students how to teach themselves.

For a long time I resisted the entreaties of one of my students, Adrienne Liebman, to write about my teachings. Writing for me is the antithesis of improvisation. Sitting alone writing and rewriting passages, clarifying and editing ideas without anyone watching and listening does not really suit my personality. The self-judging editor emerges as I write slowing me down to a frustrating crawl of words as I try to express myself through this medium of communication. It has taken me six years to complete the book, and, despite the difficulty I had doing it, I now look upon those six years as one of the more nourishing chapters in my life. Writing has helped me to clearly see the valuable structures that have emerged from my teaching over the past forty years.

I now understand why improvisation has been so important to me not just in the performance space but in my movement through life. I once described myself in a program note as an unreasonable person, someone who dislikes mulling over various options before making a decision. Even those most important decisions that affect the rest of our lives I made instantaneously with a heartfelt surety that everything would be all right. Without considering whether the choices were reasonable ones, my selections of occupation, where I live and whom I married, were done impulsively. By the way, in case you're wondering, I have been married to the same woman for twenty-three years, continue to enjoy my work forty years down the track and wouldn't live anywhere else on the planet.

Within this book the evolving style and philosophy of my work reflects my love of improvisation. The teaching itself is improvised. I haven't planned a class since I stopped teaching dance technique in September 1971. My belief that performance, especially improvised performance, should be for everyone, not just professionals, was forged in the early years of seeking out a way of teaching dance technique through improvisation. Eventually I moved away from technique and began teaching improvisation as a performing art for its own sake. It is a wonderful way to express who we are, how we are and what we do. Today all my classes contain a mix of ordinary nine to five workers, unemployed people and professional performers.

Essentially, my pedagogy enacts my belief in the fundamental principle that we all learn from each other — students from teachers, beginners from professionals, professionals from beginners, teachers from students, students from students — while my aim is to stimulate and help people evolve skills that enable them to generate spontaneous theatre with the coherence of a well-rehearsed play.

But why improvise? Why not just do a well-rehearsed play, dance piece or music composition if the intention is to have it received as if it was well rehearsed? This is a question I have asked myself many times. The writing of this book has helped me answer that question in a more meaningful way than the initial childlike indulgence of doing it because I like doing it.

One of the aspects that determines the quality of a performance is the minimisation of theatrical moments which are cumbersome or boring. Scripted, composed and choreographed performances go through a long process of development: rehearsing, editing, and refining. Everyone involved in the production works diligently to improve the show up to, and in many cases beyond, the opening night. Finally the audience arrives with an expectation of seeing a polished performance and would be quite disappointed if there were too many rough edges.

Owing to its nature, improvised performance attracts an audience, which is equally, if not more interested in the performer's skill to create the content they are presenting. The polished faultless performance plays second fiddle to the wit and ingenuity of the improvising performer. Imagine being present at a performance that has all the attributes of good theatre: a well-developed structure, interesting dialogue, exquisite movement, delightful humour and insightful social commentary. Would you not appreciate the performance more knowing that it had been totally improvised? I know I laugh heartily when a friend tells me a good joke, yet I find even more delight in a witty remark that spontaneously emerges during the course of a conversation. Being present at the moment of creation heightens the emotional impact. That is why I am so fond of attending and performing improvised theatre.

I delight in the unpredictable, love delving into the unknown, value learning through experimentation and take great pleasure in turning people on to the wonder of improvisation.

Al Wunder

1
IN THE BEGINNING

*'When I was born they cut off my right leg. This was the beginning of my dance
career. I started singing after I failed my first hearing test'.*[2]

My life as a teacher of improvisation had an unexpected beginning. I have searched my memory for the earliest event that led me here through modern dance. Boredom!! That's what started me on my career path. The boredom of a fifteen year old who hung around home annoying his mother with the slothful meandering of an unfocused 1950's New York teenager.

'Why don't you go out tonight', my mother said, 'The youth center is open. Stop moping around. Go on. It will do you good to get out of the house'. It's not that I remember the exact words forty years down the track. It is just that the acquiescence to my mother's plea to get out of the house and visit the Flushing Youth Center was the small event that led to the big event that helped put me on the path to becoming what I am today.

Nothing important happened that evening. I became acquainted with a guy whose name is lost somewhere in the recesses of my brain. The following week, however, he asked me if I would like to join him and two other girls our age and go to the movies. I agreed to this blind date and fell in love for the first time. Her name was Barbara Walter. She was to be the major catalyst for my total involvement in dance, one of two people and four lucky breaks that eventually guided me towards improvisation.

The second person, Teddy Spagna, lived in my immediate neighbourhood. On our block, 197th Street, there were several kids around the same age. We had grown up together and during our teenage years spent summer evenings dancing to the latest pop music in each other's basements. I loved this type of dancing the Phily Lindy, the Cha Cha, the Mambo, and was quite good at it. Teddy, however, was really good. We had a friendly rivalry going.

---

[2] A metaphor I used in one of my improvisations.

At that time in New York City there was a very popular TV dance program called the "Allan Freed Show". It was just a half-hour of kids boogie dancing in a television studio. The weekly dance contest was a highlight of the show. Teddy entered the contest and came in first. He was such a hit they invited him back a couple of times to show off his style. It was about a year later that Teddy introduced me to modern dance.

The four breaks happened to my right leg. It is only in hindsight that I euphemistically call these my lucky breaks. I was eight years old when I broke my leg for the first time. Myself and a third grade classmate sneaked out of school during lunch hour. He wanted to show me how he could jump from a three-metre platform onto the grass-covered ground below. After watching him do this three times I decided to have a go myself. Bad choice. Broken shinbone. Six weeks in a plaster cast, hobbling around on crutches.

Four years later I was playing with a friend in my back yard. I was watching him jump from the steps leading from the backyard to the basement. A smallish jump. Four steps if I remember correctly. There was a bit of length to negotiate however, a gap of one meter between the first and second steps. He jumped and came up smiling, I jumped and went down crying. I had broken my right thighbone. Three months in a body cast extending from my chest, down my right leg, around the ankle and up to the toes of my right foot. Totally bed ridden. Bed pans and piss bottles.

The bone did not heal right. There was a fairly acute angle at the top of the femur, a bone that should really be very straight. So when I went roller skating two years later, hit a stone and fell down, my thighbone broke for the second time. They put me in a bigger cast. Chest to right toes and down to the left knee with a bar keeping my legs at a permanent distance from each other. Another four months of bedpans and piss bottles.

X-rays showed that the bone was still at the same weird angle. Three months after returning to school I was playing basketball in the schoolyard. I went up for a rebound and came down, snapping the right femur for the third time. I became a guinea pig. A new method for dealing with fractured femurs was tried our on me. Inserting a centimetre wide pin through the entire length of the thighbone allowed for the bone to heal straight this time. I still had to spend another three months doing the bed pan and piss bottle bit with another body cast decorating half my body.

The experiment worked, and I emerged from the white plaster cocoon with a straight thighbone, never (touch wood) to be broken again. The years of immobility and inactivity had resulted in a shortened and much weakened right leg. Six months of physical therapy did help a little. Suffice to say the kids on the block started calling me "Gympie", though in a good-natured way.

To tie these three events together: the feeling between Barbara, that blind date I fell in love with, and myself was not mutual. Oh she liked me well enough but for three years from the ages of fifteen through eighteen there were times when she would go out with me and times when she wouldn't. My desires were constant, however, and the emotional roller coaster ride of acceptance and denial was very upsetting for someone who had fallen in love for the first time. The differences between us were aesthetic, cultural and intellectual. She was one of the top students in the school who loved live theatre, good music and going to art galleries, a culture vulture in other words. I also happened to think she was absolutely gorgeous.

My interests at the time consisted of going to the movies or ten-pin bowling followed by an exotic meal of pizza or Chinese food. I was also one of the best under-achieving students in our high school, scoring well in intelligence tests and struggling to maintain a C minus grade in classroom work. We didn't match up too well. I kept chasing her for four years and she neither totally accepted nor rejected me as we moved through our high school years together.

It was in the spring of my senior year that Teddy Spagna told me about a dance class that he had begun attending. Modern Dance he called it. He showed me some of the exercises and movements they did in the classes and suggested that I give it a try, his theory being that it would be great for my leg and that I'd have fun into the bargain. The name of the man he was doing classes with was José Limón, a fairly well known modern dance choreographer of the time.

The thought intrigued me and I decided to give it a go. When I told Barbara, who happened to be in an "all right I'll go out with you mood", she said she was doing the modern dance thing too and had been doing it in fact for three years every Saturday in Lower Manhattan. She was in a special advanced class for talented students (naturally), studying with a teacher by the name of Murray Louis who was the lead dancer in the Alwin Nikolais Company. Did I detect a bit of a sparkle in her eyes as we spoke about modern dance?

Consciously I was going to be very fair. I decided to go and see both the José Limón and Alwin Nikolais companies perform to see which I liked better. Then I would choose which one to take classes from. But down deep inside where my two legs fork away from the trunk of my body the decision had already been made. Good choice!!!! Actually I found I liked this thing called modern dance for itself. And fortunately Nikolais' choreography interested me more than Limon's.

Being an audience member I must admit did not cause any great stirring in me to want to become a dancer. Nor did doing an hour and a half dance technique class at Nikolais' school. I was enjoying this form of movement well enough and it did help to strengthen my right leg. Proving myself in the sporting arena was still very important to me and dancing was helping me become a better handball player, an activity I took up in high school. I had made the varsity team but was last man on a squad of thirteen. Only seven players played in a match so I rarely played in the actual competitions. I couldn't move fast enough around the court. Though I was now in my first year of university I still liked to play pick-up games in the local park and I started giving some stiff competition to the local hot shots. For those of you who don't know the game of handball it is similar to squash except you hit the ball with your hands instead of a racquet. The New York City version was an outdoor game that used one wall instead of the four-wall indoor version played in most of the other states.

I found myself enjoying life more than I had for a long time. Even my relationship with Barbara was picking up. She was going out with me fairly regularly now though she was seeing this other guy who in today's vernacular would be called a Hunk. He had been the lead trumpet player in the school band, voted best looking male of the senior class etc. etc. etc. Modern dance classes gave us some common ground to talk about and there was the possibility of being in the same class when she joined the adult evening section after her graduation from high school.

In the second semester of classes at Nikolais' I started doing both the Tuesday night technique class and the three-hour technique and theory class on a Thursday. In the theory section of class they did something called improvisation. We were given parameters such as making five different shapes and told to create short movement phrases between these shapes. On the first Thursday evening I attended this class, which was in February 1962, I did a two-minute long improvisation and it totally changed my life. I was hooked immediately, addicted to something I didn't understand. All I knew was the immense joy and power I felt. I had to have another hit. In fact I had to have many hits so, after very little agonizing over the practicalities of higher education and economic reality, I dropped out of university in June and started the professional day classes with Nikolais. This was five days a week of technique and theory. This was five days a week of improvising. This was where repeated fractures to my leg, a blind date, and some boogie dancing in Queens had led me. This was heaven.

Nikolais was to become my mentor for the next eight years. Interestingly my romance/obsession with Barbara came to an unexpected end. The summer before I was to begin my training as a professional dancer Barbara had made the decision that I was the right guy for her. For eight hot steamy days there was some heavy petting going on in the back seat of my sister's 1956 Plymouth. But something had also changed in my feelings for Barbara. The passion and desire for her had suddenly disappeared and I didn't know why. The only thing my very mixed up mind could come up with was that she had started to wear make-up and I didn't like the taste of her lipstick. This seemed trivial as a reason for the change.

I still don't understand the real basis for the loss of the passionate love I felt for someone I had worshipped for four years, hoping that some day she would fall in love with me. I've called it the X factor. I went from being an uncultured teenager to devoting my life to teaching in the performing arts. Barbara went on to university where she began majoring in psychology. She came to see me perform in a Nikolais dance piece two years after we split up. That was the last I heard from her. I always imagined she finished her degree, married, had children and is living somewhere in suburbia USA. Did she? I sometimes wonder where she is now and where I would have been if we had never met.

I am the standing one on the right

THE NIKOLAIS YEARS
Understanding what one learns is more important than what is being taught.

Alwin Nikolais

I was twenty years old when I moved out of my parents' home. My first year of professional classes with Nikolais was an even greater boon than I'd hoped for. I hadn't known it at the time but Nik (everyone called Nikolais 'Nik') would watch me dancing during my Thursday night classes. Male dancers were in short supply and Nik was planning to do a choreographic piece that would use a large group of over twenty dancers. So with less than fifty hours of dance training under my belt I found myself in Nikolais' dance company, rehearsing for my first public performance. The days were long and I was totally immersed in this wonderful world of creative culture. Perhaps it was luck but looking back I feel it was fate that he began this project the year I started dancing five days a week.

My time was totally devoted to various aspects of dance: technique, improvisation, composition, assistant teaching, and even being a techie back stage, assisting with running the lights. I was not only doing the Monday through Friday 10am to 1pm technique and theory classes but also rehearsing 2pm to 5pm each day. One day a week was given over to composition another to pedagogy. Nik wanted everyone to become the complete artist. You were encouraged to go beyond just being a dancer, to choreograph and teach as well as strut your stuff on stage.

Al Wunder Virginia Laidlaw Sandra Garner Norman Ader Lyn Levine

He used improvisation as a means to help us find material for our dance compositions, or as a way of gaining a better understanding and control over the use of time, shape, space and motion, the aesthetic colours in a dancer's palette. We also improvised movements within choreographic structures. We did not, however, perform improvisation for its own sake. In fact I got some very strange looks from fellow dancers when I said that I enjoyed watching the good classroom improvs more than a Nikolais concert. But that's the way I was, extremely excited by the moment of spontaneous invention and a bit bored by the well developed, polished product.

The Henry Street Settlement Playhouse, where Nikolais spent most of his time teaching and choreographing, was at the  time a beautiful little theatre in the Lower East Side of Manhattan. It had a lovely foyer, with two doorways opening to aisles that divided the seating on the ground floor into three sections. There was another door on the left-hand side and a small balcony only four rows deep. All 350 seats were deep-cushioned and covered in red velvet. During the 1930s/40s this was the place to go to see good avant-garde theatre; in the fifties and sixties people came to watch Nikolais' brilliant avant-garde choreography.

The Playhouse was just one of several buildings owned by the Henry Street Settlement, an organisation that offered a range of social services to the community. Every Saturday over six hundred children aged between five and eighteen would come from all over New York City and descend on Grand and Henry Streets to attend drama and dance classes. Several classes were run simultaneously in various classrooms spread among the several buildings that made up the settlement. Obviously, many teachers were needed. As part of our training, we students doing the professional classes were expected to apprentice ourselves to another teacher. For my first two years I worked with Phyllis Lamhut, one of Nikolais' principal dancers. The following two years I taught young children on my own, using Nikolais' technique and improvisation. Thus began my professional career: I was earning enough money from my teaching to cover a quarter of my tuition fees with Nikolais. An interesting conundrum, paying the master to teach me how to teach so that I could earn enough money to continue studying with him!

Some major changes occurred during my fourth year at the Playhouse. Nik's choreography was becoming a hot item not only in New York but nationally and internationally as well. His company was in demand across the United States and Europe. In 1966 he was away on his first major European tour when I approached Betty Young, the executive director of the Playhouse. I asked rather tentatively if she would check with Nik about the possibility of my teaching one of the adult-beginners dance classes, telling her that I thought I would like teaching adults more than children. She laughed and said that was great. It seems Nikolais, who was extending his tour in Europe, would not be in New York when the first semester started in September and wanted me to teach some of the professional classes. I stared at Betty. I might have even gaped. I kept gaping, finally offering some words to the effect that I had no experience in teaching adults. That I was arguably the poorest dancer in the school. Betty smiled at me and just kept on smiling as I rambled on about my inadequacies. However it was an offer I couldn't refuse. The money received from this additional teaching would completely cover the tuition I would have to pay when Nik was back in town and teaching.

My worst fears about being totally inexperienced and taking on the responsibility of teaching dance to people who were better dancers than me paled in comparison to the reality of confronting an eager room full of them. I did not know these people. They were strangers, hot-shot dancers from all over the United States who had seen Nikolais' company perform during its national tour the previous year. Having participated in a master class taught by Nikolais himself, they had come to New York to study with the master or at least one of the members of his company. None of them knew they were the first adults I would teach. Five out of twenty students walked out of class before it was finished. Not the best beginning, not the best beginning at all.

I spoke with Nik a couple of times during the year, almost begging him to relieve me from teaching the professional classes. He didn't really listen to my anxieties about incompetence and always talked me out of my desire to quit, saying he had faith in me and not to worry about the ones who walked out. I still believe that having me teach was just a circumstance he had to deal with. The sudden demand for him and his company to tour around the world for half the year was his reward for the decades he had spent developing his artistry. He deserved the fame and fortune that was now coming his way. So off he went, taking with him all the other experienced teachers who were members of his dance company, leaving myself and two other students to teach the professional classes in his absence.

It was a trying year. I struggled to keep my confidence at a level that would allow me just to walk into class. It was near the end of the year when something positive occurred. I taught something I hadn't learnt from Nikolais. I presented a set of parameters for an improvisation that was an invention of my own. It was a simple group score devised for quintets. I asked the groups of five to begin from a point of stillness, for each dancer to maintain a slightly uncomfortable shape, and to be absolutely still for as long as possible. The first movement, when someone could no longer stand being still, was to be explosive. The other dancers were to respond immediately, equally explosively. Every single one of the four quintets was exciting, fun and aesthetically pleasing for both doers and watchers. My first original thought as a teacher had turned out to be a good one. The idea came out of nowhere, unplanned, it was improvised teaching of improvisation and it worked. For the remainder of my student years at Henry Street Playhouse I continued to choreograph and teach, concentrating on developing the innovative approaches I would need for my life's work with improvisation.

During my years of study at the Playhouse two comments in particular would greatly influence my future teaching style. The first was by Nikolais' lead dancer, Murray Louis, whom I considered a brilliant teacher. Nikolais' strength as an instructor was in presenting the technical intricacy and related philosophies of his practice. Murray on the other hand remains one of the most entertaining speakers I have ever listened to. The information was still there but couched in language that had me chuckling as well as comprehending. His words inspired me to throw myself whole-heartedly into the exercises. I became more emotionally involved in pursuing the movement pattern or improvising within the parameters given by Murray than I did with Nikolais. Nik's words and style of presentation were designed to enlighten, to give understanding to the principles involved in making dance a communicative art. Murray got me doing it with panache.

The words in question occurred one Sunday afternoon while he was holding court between the matinee and evening performances of Nikolais' dance piece 'Sanctum'. Murray always seemed to be the centre of attention wherever he was, but especially among us student dancers, teaching even when he wasn't supposed to be. The topic was teaching dance. "If you can't talk you can't teach", he told us. This statement initially scared me since I still felt very inadequate in verbal conversation but ultimately it helped me to focus on and clarify my use of language as a teacher. Whereas Murray used lots of entertaining similes, taking two to three minutes to explain an exercise, I will construct a two or three sentence score that sets some very clear parameters yet purposefully leaves lots of space for student input and interpretation. My words are sparse. I don't explain what makes a movement interesting but use vocabulary to intrigue, to inspire experimentation, letting students find the interesting movement on their own. What I most want to teach is for students to trust and develop their own self-teacher who can speak intelligently about style, practice and aesthetics. I believe we are our own best teachers but unfortunately have fallen into the trap of listening to gurus, following only their pathway to enlightenment and losing faith in seeking our own way to understanding.

It was a second comment from a good friend and fellow dancer Bob Beswick which has influenced my non-teaching teaching style even more than Murray's words. He once described Nikolais' technique as the whitest among all the major dance teachers. What he meant by this is that the technique did not require a precise adherence to form but engendered an exploration into physical and aesthetic principles of movement and theatre. This development through exploration allowed for individual styles to emerge. A variety of strong, vibrant and unique dancers evolved from it, individuals whose one common denominator was their articulation of movement, the ability to speak their non-verbal dance language with skill. Four of Nik's principle dancers, Murray Louis, Gladys Bailin, Phyllis Lamhut and Bill Frank are excellent examples, and each had their own strength and style of dancing.

Phyllis Lamhut   Murray Louis   Gladys Bailin

Murray was the Frank Sinatra of dance. His physical technique was just adequate but the nuance, colour and wit of his physical phrasing was outstanding. Gladys was small and had a smooth, sensuous and easeful quality of motion. Beauty was her middle name. Phyllis also small in stature but wiry, strong and direct in quality, was the best physical comedian of the lot.

Bill, an African-American, was like a living Rodin sculpture. His physical presence commanded instant attention. Over six feet tall, face and body beautifully chiselled, his movements were big, strong and athletically graceful. One could easily believe that these four had studied with different teachers, which was not the case at all. It was Nik's white technique' that allowed these four to develop the styles that so suited their personalities.

Bill Frank and Gladys Bailin

During the eight years I spent dancing, teaching and performing at the Henry Street Playhouse I absorbed much of value from Nik. There is, however, very little resemblance between what

I learned from him and what I teach. I do not teach what he taught. I teach what I learned. Nik would talk about time, shape, space and motion, as being the building blocks of choreography. All our improvisations and choreographic studies evolved around these elements. I no longer teach time, shape, space and motion as such, and haven't done so since 1971. However, it is the breaking down of an area of research into three or four building blocks that has become the essence of my teaching. I look at an area of movement that I wish to research then break it down into smaller sub-areas.

After I had been teaching the professional workshops for a few years students were no longer walking out in the middle of class. I was more trusting of my own ideas, coming up with diverse improvised scores to play with. I was also doing a fair amount of choreography and my theatrical and emotionally-based pieces were quite successful. The pieces dealing with pure dance steps however, were, frankly, terrible.

By 1969 I had the feeling that I should be doing something else. Being a somewhat insular person however, I did not have the curiosity nor the spirit to seek out new things. Bob Beswick had been telling me about some very interesting dance explorations taking place in Judson Church which was being used as a rehearsal hall by dancers such as James Dunn, Yvonne Rainer, Steve Paxton and others and can arguably be called the birthplace of post-modern dance. People were actually performing improvisation and he thought I might like to see what was happening. But I had been too immersed in my life at Henry Street, never really venturing out to see what the rest of the dance world was doing.

Nevertheless my deepening friendship with Bob was to have unexpected consequences. He would be directly responsible for my leaving New York City and moving to San Francisco, the next great change in my life and the most important decision I have ever made. So to you Bob, wherever you are, I offer you my heartfelt thanks for getting me to look beyond the boundaries of the house I lived within.

Al Wunder   Bob Beswick

3

GOING TO SAN FRANCISCO

I added up the number of days I had gone beyond the city limits. Granted New York City is a big city but I was astounded that the total was less than three hundred and sixty-five. I was twenty-six years old and had spent less than one year of that time beyond the confines of the city boundary. This included visiting my sister and aunt who lived on Long Island and in New Jersey respectively.

Part of the tally were the vacations I spent in the Catskills, a small mountain range seventy-five miles north of New York City, with my family in the summers between 1948 and 1953. So when Bob Beswick asked me if I wanted to co-teach a summer workshop in San Francisco I immediately replied in the affirmative.

This upcoming moneymaking vacation plan initiated my looking back at my lack of travel experience. I was very insular as I said earlier. I thought I would check out the scene. Wow man!! I was already talking like a Californian hippie.

The second day after my arrival on the West Coast I called my parents and friends and told them to send my things over, I wasn't coming back to New York. I had fallen in love again. This time with a place, a place that had trees and grass. A place where pedestrians were given the right of way pleasantly by motor cars. A place where people wore flowers in their hair and where happiness far outweighed anger.

Another sudden big change in my life thoughtlessly, recklessly done, proving once again that my impulsive behaviour is a valuable resource.

I spent the next twelve years, 1970-1982, experimenting with and developing my work in improvisation. My initial explorations dealt mainly with teaching dance technique through improvisation. I wanted to eliminate the set exercises, eight bounces over the right leg, eight over the left, eight centre, and so on. Doing away with the pliés and set routines across the floor was also important to me. Replacing the routines with movement that stayed within certain parameters was my method for getting people to work on physical skills without repetitive exercises. The first score I put out to students was 'open and close the space between your head and your shoulders', an improvisational exercise designed to increase flexibility in the neck and upper torso. The concept was simple: it allowed students to work creatively on stretching various muscles without the regimentation of set exercises. Gradually I also found ways to develop strength, balance and body alignment through creative play. Today the results of this work can be glimpsed in the first thirty minutes of my class, the personal physical play (warm-ups). I'll spend a lot more time on this subject later but first some background about my initial year of teaching in San Francisco

The workshop that Bob and I taught was a huge success. People wanted us to stay on and teach there. I almost but couldn't quite convince Bob to do this. He was after all in the Nikolais Dance Company and would be travelling around Europe getting paid for doing what he loved. I had already made up my mind to stay. In the fall of 1970 I started up my own dance studio in downtown San Francisco.

Things got off to a great start. I followed Nikolais' format of three-hour classes taught five times a week, scheduling these to run from 10am to 1pm. There were rehearsal times in the afternoon and I also taught two evening classes a week. Very full on. I was still teaching Nikolais' technique and theory. This consisted of stretching exercises, plies and combinations across the floor. Some original ideas of my own evolved in the improvisation section of class that year. Two that spring to mind are the *activated nouns* and *ignored partner* scores.

The *activated noun* parameter was image based. I instructed students to dance to phrases such as 'hyperactive steel wool' or 'lazy thighbones'. I have rarely used imagery as part of my teaching but this particular form of verbal suggestion provided students with a humorous way to discover and produce a movement vocabulary that was different from what they would normally choose, was extremely varied and was without stylistic modern dance overtones. The perfect execution of turns, leaps and leg extensions quite frankly bored me. My aesthetics of dance already had me looking towards the development of a way of moving that expressed one's personality in an imaginative way.

A second score that I thoroughly enjoyed was setting up duets in which partners were to avoid looking directly at each other. This created very unusual and quite beautiful shape relationships between two people who, while purposely refusing visual acknowledgment, nevertheless were very conscious of the spatial relationship between them. Looking for new ways of doing old things once again produced unexpected and exciting results. Initially I simply wanted to see what would happen if duet partners did not try to relate to each other but did their own thing while making sure they were not influenced by what their partner was doing. The act of 'purposely ignoring' already makes for a very strong connection. This purposeful avoidance of making a connection with someone seemed to create an invisible energy bond between the two students. A whole new range of duet shape possibilities emerged. There was rarely the direct front to front, front to back, or side to side relationships that so predominate our way of relating spatially. Instead the shapes were unusual with facings and angles that seemed to defy each other, an asymmetry that created intrigue, tension and even humour — the interest of the relationship being in the differences rather than the similarities, in the disjointed rather than the cohesive, in the unusual rather than the usual.

After several months of teaching seven three-hour classes a week my energy started to slump. No new ideas came to me for the technique part of class. The dance exercises and combinations across the floor were becoming repetitious and boring. Even my improvisation scores were lacking inspiration. Students began dropping out of class. My first attempt at being a totally independent dance teacher started looking very shaky.

By the end of the year my income could no longer cover expenses. I was a failure but, being a person whose persistence far-outweighed diligence, I refused to give up. Fortunately two students, Terry Sendgraff and Ruth Zaporah, brought something very special to classes. Terry was a well-trained gymnast and modern dancer whose positive spirit and natural inquisitiveness inspired everyone in class. Ruth even to this day remains the most natural improviser to pass through my workshops. Her ability to stay in the present and be impulsive while still maintaining a high

Al Wunder   Terry Sendgraff   Ruth Zaporah

quality theatrical aesthetic made her a unique performer.

I asked these two if they would combine with me in a joint venture of teaching and creating performances. To my great delight they said "Yes" and the Berkeley Dance Theatre & Gymnasium was born. This was the real beginning of my research into improvisation as an entity unto itself and not just a part of a dance class.

We found a small space above a Chinese grocer just over
the Bay Bridge from San Francisco in Berkeley, California. I had
to build walls and lay down a particle-board floor. We were there
for one year before moving into a beautiful space on Parker Street
in Berkeley. Here I tore down several walls and sanded back a
gorgeous wooden floor. I believe the space is still being run as a
dance studio today. One of the legacies I left behind.

The three of us were choreographing and teaching,
building up a student base of about twenty people. There was a
group of ten students who regularly attended classes, a wonderful
mix of professionals and non-professionals, which provided a
combination of expertise and uninhibited creativity. This
professional/non-professional combination created such a
productive atmosphere that to this day I still refuse to organise
workshops around the beginner, intermediate and advanced model
but rather maintain a multi-level structure in all my classes.

If the muse can really sing she was singing beautifully for
me. I had no idea where my ideas were coming from. Every class
I taught worked superbly. I was creating an improvised way of
teaching technique as well as helping people to be impulsive and
playful whilst learning something about dance choreography.

My concepts came from an internal source without any
obvious connection to what I had learned from Nikolais. Looking
back now I can see that I was intuitively choosing areas I wanted to
work on, creating in the process a set of parameters for students to
explore. Initially I took the set exercises and across the floor
combinations I learned from Nik and turned them into improvised
movement experiences. Stretching the hamstrings by reaching over
the legs while sitting with them straight in front of you, became
'open and close the space between head and feet.' Another way
people can stretch these thigh muscles is to straighten and bend the
knees in a standing position letting the natural weight of head and
arms hang over the legs.

Most dance teachers used combinations across the floor to
help develop various dance techniques. Turns, leaps and balances
were incorporated into a sequence of movements with varying

degrees of difficulty. The good dancers quickly learned the routine and smiled elegantly as they gracefully moved across the room. The not so good hoofers frowned and muttered as they muffed a turn and lost balance while trying to execute the given dance steps. I wanted to do away with the goal of perfecting certain routines since this set up a competition which created a hierarchy of the good, the not so good and the no-hopers. My own technical dance ability fell somewhere in between the last two categories yet my choreographic and improvising skills would have been in the top classification. Also, there were other students like me whose physical attributes did not fit the stylistic criteria of the day. But I loved watching them dance anyway. There was something about their individuality, movements that came from the heart rather than the "perfect body" that touched me in a way the best dance technicians couldn't.

My teaching began to reflect my personal view of what I enjoyed in a dancer. I did not create a movement sequence for students to copy but would direct them to find their own ways of walking, jumping, turning and stopping as they travelled across the room. One of the methods I used to help students explore turns was to draw their attention to the fact that, while turning, half of the body (right or left) moves forward as the other half moves backwards. It is similar to a revolving door. Try to imagine your spine is the axis of the door and that the right and left sides of your body are the door panels rotating around it. By making sure that when the right side of your body is going forward the left side is moving at an equal speed backwards you reduce resistance to the direction of your turn and it becomes much easier to do.

I had begun to deal with basics. It was the beginning of a styleless marriage between dancers and their art. Everyone was invited to create his or her own way of working on technique. Flexibility was achieved through the awareness and play of opening and closing the spaces between various body parts. For example by opening and closing the space between your shoulders and ears you will be stretching the tendons of the neck, increasing mobility in the shoulder joints and opening up the muscles in your upper torso.

Extending this idea further by getting students to open and close the space between fingernails and the walls and ceiling brought a twisting motion into play which engaged various muscles throughout the torso, lengthening and strengthening them. Incorporating the concept of allowing the body to roll into various sitting positions while extending and swinging their arms helped students to find creative ways of stretching the spine, lower backs, hip joints and leg muscles. Extending the hips towards and away from the floor or towards and away from the ceiling allowed for deeper flexibility work in the spine. This was the thrust of my initial exploration of teaching dance technique through improvisation. I did away with the formula of set positions and set number of repetitions, substituting concepts and awareness of movement possibilities which come from feeling the kinaesthetic and spatial relationships between different body parts.

But simply substituting awareness and play for exercises wasn't quite enough for me. I wanted to establish a general sense of inquisitiveness about dance and dance technique. What are the elements that make up a good dance technique? What makes for a good dancer? What is important to you as a performer? There is no right or wrong answer to these questions, rather they're a check list for anyone interested in developing their own unique dance or movement style.

I had students look at the dynamics of muscle flexibility. What causes muscles to stretch? I put forward the theory that muscles do not have the capacity to stretch; that the only physical action a muscle can achieve on its own is contraction. So we eliminated the word 'stretching' from our vocabulary and spoke of expanding muscles by relaxing them and using either gravity, or other muscle groups, or another person gently pushing or pulling you, to help increase flexibility.

Then there is the rubber band analogy. Pulling on one end cannot stretch a rubber band. The other end has to be held in order for the extension to happen. From this awareness came the concept of the *motion point* and *resistance point*. An example of this is the dancer who wants to work on flexibility of the spine. The dancer could choose the top of the head as the motion point then gradually move the resistance point down the spine from the shoulders to the shoulder blades, to the middle back, to the hip joint. As the resistance point moves lower down the spine more of the torso and its various muscle groups can come into play, being moved and elongated. By switching the motion and resistance points around – that is, letting the top of the head be the resisting point and the hip the motion point – some unusual movements occur. You could even declare the middle of the spine as your motion point with the top and or bottom of the spine as resistance points. Or what happens if the resistance point is in the feet with the motion point being the chin?

What has occurred is that the students now combine physical skill development with creative play. They are making decisions about how much flexibility or strength or balance work they want to do. Each student chooses how they want to divide the amount of time spent on creative playfulness and physical discipline.

I worked on the premise that it is the playful repetition of enjoyable movements which allows the developmental aspect of physicality to progress. The idea is that by doing a greater variety of movements with a similar goal (hamstring flexibility for example), the student can develop a larger motional vocabulary than by constantly repeating the same movement pattern. By using this creative approach to skill development I hoped dancers would access a movement language that they were emotionally involved with. I call this the other half of technique. This is the half that gives life to movement, the emotion to motion connection that enhances the communication value of physical language.

I realised that my new style of teaching technique would not produce the so-called good technical dancer. It could, however, turn a good physical technician into a very good performer and similarly enhance the aesthetic qualities of a less athletic dancer. What this other half of technique did was to make dancers more aware of and more responsible for their own personal development. I wanted them to begin thinking about what they wanted to do as performers - what skills they wanted to develop and what possible strategies they might put in place to develop those skills?

The process my teaching took was the search for an ever-increasing movement vocabulary which helps develop flexibility, strength, speed, balance and coordination. It also formed the basis of my philosophy of teaching, inspiring students to become their own best teachers.

The physical play, non-exercise-based technique work, took place in the first half-hour of my class. Students worked on their own, within the body-part spatial parameters I gave them, concentrating on personal physical development. The next hour was spent travelling across the floor. This was the time when locomotion skills were enhanced. We played with turns, balances, leaps and all manner of intricate use of legs and feet. Moving across the floor three abreast allowed for sharing different ways of executing turns and balances with each other, sometimes copying movements of the person coming across the floor next to you sometimes offering your own variation.

The last part of my classes was improvisation for its own sake. It was in this section of class that we looked at group scores which facilitated theatrical relationships and communication involving three or more people. Some of my early work on the use of vision began with exploring the ways a dancer can look at his or her partners. This included extremely close looking, looking from far away, looking from unusual positions, direct looking, using peripheral vision and unsighted looking. This simple act of exploring the way we look and see opened up new pathways to how we  feel and experience movements. With the emphasis now on looking rather than on 'looking good', movement vocabulary had a fresher more creative and playful look.

Actually seeing what is looked at is in itself a valuable exercise, a wonderful way of bringing the self into the present. One of the several scores I invented on this theme was to point behind yourself then turn and name in a single word what you saw. Doing this to a drumbeat that began very slowly and gradually picked up speed developed not only the students' ability to stay in the present but also quickness in finding descriptive words. Interestingly this was one of my first forays into the use of combining language and movement. I enjoyed the challenge of adding the cognitive to the kinaesthetic and, many years later, combining words and movement became an integral part of my teaching.

My teaching had already changed drastically from what I had learned during my years with Alwin Nikolais. The improvisational way of teaching dance through improvisation and its appeal to the dancer and non-dancer alike attracted many students to our Parker Street Studio. Ruth, Terry and I choreographed dance pieces that were performed in small studios around the San Francisco Bay Area. We were gaining a good reputation for our work and began sharing ideas and working with other artists. Then without any warning my muse stopped singing. Suddenly, one evening, she just left.

I remember the night but not the date. I had decided not to play my own musical accompaniment as I usually did for the thirty minute-long, large group improv, which had recently become the closing section of my classes. Instead I put on a tape of old music scores that I had used for several of my New York choreographic pieces. It was a disaster. No one, including myself, enjoyed the improvisation that followed. Of course this event would not have been the cause but it certainly seemed to be the catalyst for my teaching losing its creative freshness. I didn't understand nor could I alter this loss of inspiration and confidence. Student numbers began to dwindle. New ideas fell flat so I tried repeating previous material. This didn't work either. I struggled on for another year but eventually had to stop teaching.

I entered a phase that lacked direction and purpose. Three things kept me sane and allowed me to cope: Terry, Ruth and Hum Drums. Terry and I had been lovers, living together through the initial success of the Berkeley Dance Theatre & Gymnasium. Now she became my teacher, one of several people who started off being students of mine only to become my tutors. I began doing her gymnastics classes, and was fairly good at the basic tumbling techniques. At the height of my gymnastic prowess I was able to do forward and backward rolls, handstands and cartwheels, head stands, round-offs, back rolls into head and hand stands, flying cart-wheels, and forward dive rolls. I was never able to master the back handspring, back flip or aerial cartwheel. I thoroughly enjoyed the new expanded movement vocabulary this work gave me. Yet the most important thing I learned from Terry came not from her teaching but from living with her. Her need to express feelings and my lack of being able to verbally express mine was to become a sore point in our relationship. It was actually dealing with this difference in the communication of feelings between us that lead me towards a major change in the way I related to people. The cause of this change helped to form the basis for *Positive Feedback*, the most important aspect of my future teaching in Melbourne. I will discuss this cause and *Positive Feedback* in the chapter, *Eye to Eye*.

Just after her fortieth birthday, Terry began experimenting with movement on a trapeze. She was moving forward in her development as a performing artist while I was moving into a very dark period in my life. Terry was interested in working with an apparatus that was low enough for her to grab onto while still standing on the ground. This low-level trapeze allowed her to create a dance form that could move from the earth to the air. It allowed her to fly, something she had always wanted to do since she was a little girl. Her strong gymnastic and modern dance training helped her to develop this uniquely beautiful form of aerial dance and teach what see called 'Motivity'. This was a combination of dance, low level trapeze work, gymnastics and just being yourself while speaking to an audience. It was a marvellous and unique combination of skills to improvise with.

Lynden Nicholls   Clover Catskill   Terry Sendgraff

Terry and I split up when she had an affair with a woman. Her discovery that she was gay both ended and enriched our relationship. We moved from being lovers to great friends. Terry had taught me how to express feelings through words. She became the friend I could talk to about the pain and anger I was feeling because of the change in our relationship. I was also able to seek out other people with whom I could speak easily and naturally about feelings that hurt and feelings that made me smile. In this way I was able to maintain a happy lifestyle though going through a period in my life where I was physically troubled and economically poor.

A torn knee cartilage and a minor herniation of a lumbar disc forced me to stop dancing. I could walk well enough but even a gentle jog of over a hundred meters would cause my back to stiffen up quite badly. Fortunately I had met Jim Nolman. He was an inter-species musician who has created music with other animals: singing with three hundred turkeys, howling with timber wolves and beating out rhythms in Death Valley, with kangaroo rats. He influenced me in a very unexpected way, setting me on a path that would lead to my becoming a musician and furniture maker.

Jim made and played a wonderful wooden drum — no animal skins, just wood, very appropriate for an inter-species musician — a rectangular wooden box with tongue-like shapes cut through the top piece of wood, hence its generic name 'Tongue Drum'. The various lengths and shapes of the tongues produced different melodic pitches. At the time I was making and selling the more usual animal skin head percussion instruments and wanted to know more about Jim's drums. He told me that they were an ancient Mayan Indian instrument and very simple to make. Just a hollow box with tongues of any shape cut through the top piece of wood. I decided to try my hand at making this amazing instrument and was able to take advantage of a cooperative woodworking space in an artists' complex in Berkeley. It was a place where people with skills taught people who wanted to learn skills. We paid a monthly fee for a small space within a large open warehouse, sharing the major woodworking tools and buying our own hand tools.

I received free instruction on the use, safety and maintenance of table saws, buzzers (a machine that creates a straight edge on a length of timber), thicknessers (this machine finishes the timber to the desired thickness) and radial arm saws (cuts timber to the required length). I also apprenticed myself to a man who taught me how to build cabinets. This was the place that I developed my *Hum Drums*, the trade name for the tongue drum that I still make and sell today. As well as economically helping to sustain me the development of *Hum Drums* plus cabinet and furniture-making became my creative outlet during the time I could not dance.

In 1980 I experienced a major herniation of the same lumbar disc. Now I couldn't even stand up without feeling the most excruciating pain. My left leg went numb from mid-calf to toes. The attending neurosurgeon said I had two options, extended bed rest or a spinal fusion operation. I chose the former and spent seven months in bed. There were no bedpans and piss bottles this time as I was allowed to go to the toilet and bathe and prepare food. I thought this was going to be the final straw that broke the

Wunder's back. My career as teacher, dancer and performer looked as if it was finally over. I hadn't been doing very much in the past few years. I made the odd unsuccessful attempts teaching movement again. I tried doing classes taught by Terry, Ruth, plus a few other teachers of improvised movement and theatre. I was doing some lighting designs for various groups and musically accompanying a few classes. I even helped to install a wooden dance floor or two. Oddly enough when I was fully recovered from my back problems I started dancing again.

Belly Dancing. What a way to loosen up a very stiff lower back! It was fun and the teacher, Jamie Miller, was great to work with. I found her organisational format of having people pay in advance for a month's classes and receiving a private session with her as part of the package to be a phenomenal teaching device. The private sessions helped me to develop my belly-dance skills quickly and the monthly payments offered a sense of ongoing commitment. I was later to use this model for my own work in Melbourne.

After I'd been belly dancing for a year Ruth Zaporah asked me to join a class of chosen students, people whose work she admired. She had developed what was called 'Action Theatre', a mix of abstract movement, gesture, character and verbal improvisation. She was an exquisite performer and excellent teacher and I couldn't turn this offer down. Ruth was another of those who became my teacher after starting off as a student. Workshopping with this group, under Ruth's guidance, helped me find my 'talking performer'. Both Terry and Ruth had found a way of using language  combined with movement and this defined their style of improvised performance while I had yet to find my theatrical voice.

The breakthrough came with a particular story. The exercise Ruth set up was for one of the group, me in this case, to sit and tell a story while the rest of the group matched their movements to it. My story was about a ten-year-old boy who is sitting in a tree. His mother is in the house with the doctor attending his very sick father and she had sent him outside to play. The boy notices a large semi-trailer driving down their country road. The trailer stops in front of the house. The large back doors open and an old man sitting in a rocking chair floats from the trailer, through the air and into the house, appearing several minutes later with the boy's father sitting on his lap. They are both laughing and talking as the rocking chair re-enters the back of the semi-trailer and proceeds on its journey. As the truck disappears around the bend the boy hears his mother scream.

For the first time I became totally immersed in improvising language. When I look back on it now I realize I had created a fantasy with as much power for me as my first movement improvisation in New York. It would take a while before I would find another story that flowed as easily as that one, but it was the beginning of using language as part of my improvisation and started me on the road to combining theatre and dance.

I watched with jealous admiration as Terry and Ruth became popular performers and teachers, attracting many students to their classes and huge audiences to their performances. They were not the only ones doing well as improvising performers and teachers. The San Francisco Bay area had become a hotbed of improvisational happenings during the 1970's.

When I first arrived on the West Coast in 1970 Anna Halprin was the only person dealing with improvisation, but within a few years there were several groups all 'doing their own thing' as we used to say back then. One of these was the Blake Street Hawkeyes, four actors exploring physically based improvised theatre. From the East Coast came 'Contact Improvisation', a new dance form that was to sweep the world with its innovative form of dance exploration. An all-male performing troupe, called Mangrove formed, experimenting with a mix of theatre, music and contact improvisation. Ruth's Action Theatre and Terry's Motivity with her performing group Fly By Night were also going strong.

Mangrove was a wonderful eclectic mix of male energy. Kurt Siddal was one of the original contact improvisers working in New York City with Steve Paxton. Jim Tyler had been a solo dancer in the Eric Hawkins Dance Company; he was also an accomplished flautist and percussionist. John LeFan performed in musicals in his home state of Texas. I had met Bob Reese in Oregon when he first started exploring dance. He was intrigued with my work in improvisation and a year later fell in love with Contact Improvisation when he came across it. Byron Brown, like Bob, was attracted to performance through this particular mode. Together they formed a unique and multi-talented group of men who taught and performed their combination of contact and theatre improvisation.

The 'Blake Street Hawkeyes' was a quartet of actors, Bob Ernst, David Shine, Cynthia Moore and John O'Keefe, who wanted to get away from the overly verbal type of conventional theatre they had studied. They were outrageous in their development of madcap characters with strong, delightfully ungraceful physicality. I was still too close to my roots as a modern dancer to appreciate totally their movement style but was in absolute awe of their ability to improvise dialogue between themselves.

Another member joined the 'Blake Street Hawkeyes' when I was laid up in bed with my herniated disc. Friends, who came to visit me at my house, told me about a wonderful black woman with an outlandish name. She was an extremely funny and talented performer they proclaimed and I had to go and see her when I got better. I did finally get to watch Whoopee Goldberg improvise a few times and also perform a scripted one-woman show just before she left for New York where fame and fortune awaited her.

The energies of these groups fostered a phenomenal growth in improvisation as an art form. Each company attracted and shared a growing number of students and audience members. Even the teachers/performers would do each other's classes, sharing the insights and techniques that we were evolving separately and in conjunction with each other. The same students could be seen doing classes with all the different teachers, gaining a broad knowledge of improvisation in the different performance disciplines.

It was when all this activity was at its height that I had sank to my low due to my back injuries. When my back improved and I still wasn't teaching or performing I became a student doing contact improvisation classes with members from Mangrove, joined in some voice and acting classes with the Blake Street Hawkeyes, jumped on and off trapezes learning Terry's Motivity and struggled with combining my movement skills with voice and words in Ruth's Action Theatre classes.

I was now studying with many artists and learning a lot about various forms of theatre and movement that were different from the dance I had learned in New York. This was the most frustrating and yet most creative time in my life. I still had the need to express feelings but I was no longer doing enough dancing and performing for that to be my language. And once again economics had become a problem so I took on a newspaper delivery route throwing over two hundred papers from my car window seven days a week. Gradually, I started teaching again and with the few students who came along had a final fling at developing dance technique through improvisation evolving what I called *The Sequence of Four*. This was a routine that embodied four sequential movement patterns designed to give the dancer a full and extensive body warm up and facilitate the further development of physical skills. It included *The Swaying*, *The Hang Over*, *The Ups and Downs*, and *A Little Bit of Rock and Roll*.

The Swaying originated when I was teaching an all-men's class. Here we were, a group of strong not so macho people with powerful but inflexible shoulder and upper torso muscles. Throughout my years with Nikolais, teachers were always telling me to pull my shoulders down so I devised an exercise where I would sway my upper body by shifting my weight slightly from foot to foot thereby causing my hips to swing. The arms hang from the shoulders, using the momentum built up from the swaying as their only impetus for moving. The concept was to eliminate muscle use in the upper torso area and get the swinging, hanging weight of the arms to elongate the shoulder and pectoral muscles.

I added a balance and turning routine to the swaying. By the simple act of lifting a knee while swaying, varying degrees of turns were accomplished, depending on the initial force of the sway. The hard thing was to keep the knee lift simple and straight in front of the body, not really thinking about the turn but letting it happen purely as a result of the swinging arms.

After several minutes of this gentle swaying and turning I had the participants just hang over their legs with their knees bent slightly so their fingertips touched the floor. We stayed in this position for a minute or two just relaxing and feeling the natural loose hanging weight of our head, torso and arms. Compared with women most men have tighter hamstrings. I found that trying to stretch my hamstrings while sitting on the floor and reaching out over straight legs tended to tighten my lower back muscles. The *Hang Over* sequence was designed to let gravity do the work while the only muscular activity I did was to gently straighten and bend my knees. Again the most difficult thing was to keep it simple. The object is to let the body hang over the legs, avoiding the desire to push muscularly closer to the ground. As knees are straightened the weight of the torso, arms and head will elongate the hamstrings. I don't try to keep my fingertips on the floor but let them ride up and down according to the level of my flexibility of the moment.

By varying the positions of feet and torso in the *Hang Over* pose the elongation process effects various muscle groups in the upper leg. A welcomed and unanticipated offshoot of this exercise was that, through gentle repetition, it also strengthened the quadriceps.

This brought us to the *Ups and Downs*. Using various body parts (head, hip, arm, hand, foot, etc.) as a primary source of movement, I had participants lift and lower themselves towards and away from the floor. The degree of lift was varied, sometimes going fully to standing, sometimes moving just a few centimetres up and down. Weight could be taken on the feet or the back, hands and feet combined, knees, shoulders or whatever body parts the student chose to use for support. This was the strengthening section of my workout. It also allowed bodies to become comfortable and creative with movements into and out of the floor.

Now we were ready to *Rock and Roll*.

Finishing the *Ups and Downs* in a down position, I put students through several minutes of rolling and sitting, getting them to vary their sitting positions, legs straight out in front, legs wide apart, both legs folded, one folded one straight, sitting on both heels, etc. As they rolled through these sitting positions the purpose was to let the weight of the head, arms and torso slowly rock over the legs. This resulted in some very deep flexibility work for the hamstrings, hip joints and lower back. It also helped in strengthening the abdominal muscles. By using these four movement sequences students could achieve a full dance work out through creative play and not have to deal with repetitious exercises.

I also created several alignment scores that took the form of walking meditations. My favourite one I call the *double gravity* image. First I had students stand and feel the amount of effort they were using to keep themselves from falling down. I then had them imagine that gravity was reversed and with the same amount of energy they used earlier to keep from falling down, they were to keep themselves from falling up. The next step was to walk around the room maintaining this reverse gravity image in their bodies. After a few minutes of this I asked them to maintain the upward fall of gravity in the spine but to let the natural downward fall of gravity effect all the other meat and bone parts of the body. If achieved, this image helps to minimise the degree of muscle tension in the shoulder and torso area, makes breathing easier, and allows for a more relaxed movement of arms and legs.

I thought I would never leave San Francisco but, for me, the love of place cannot compete with the love of a person. The meeting of my future wife was a somewhat psychic happening. My friend Terry told me one day she was going to teach a workshop in Australia. I felt this POING go off in my head. I didn't hear it, I felt it. I knew then I was going to go to Australia. I had never been more certain of anything in my whole life. When Terry returned from teaching her Motivity workshop in Melbourne she said, "A woman is coming from Australia to study with me in July, you're going to fall madly in love with her".

4

MELBOURNE TIMES

I followed my heart and left San Francisco arriving in Melbourne, Australia July 1982. The idea was to spend a few

months living with Lynden Nicholls (the woman I fell madly in love with) to see how we would get along as a defacto couple. I also wanted to see how I might earn a living from my teaching and drum making. This was the responsible me trying to take control from the gut-level, instant-decision-making me who has ruled my life since I started dancing full time in 1962. I knew the move would be permanent, but since this change of life involved another person, I had to seem as if I were acting in a reasonable manner. But I am not a reasonable person. I like reacting to quickly-made decisions more than thinking beforehand about the possible outcomes of an action. Isn't this the essence of an improviser?

On my first morning in Australia I took a walk. Rounding a corner I stood facing north, looking up Sydney Road. My eyes watered as my brain leapt backwards in time to when I was an eight-year-old in Williamsburg, Brooklyn. Sydney Road was the spitting image of Grand Street, a long busy thoroughfare with Mom and Pop stores lining both sides of the street. But I was in Melbourne, thirty years in time and over ten thousand miles in distance from the original home of my childhood. I was soon to teach my first class in Australia. Interestingly, I was not at all concerned whether this most drastic life change would prove valuable or not. I was following my heart and, true to form, this decision to start a new life half way around the world turned out to be a good one.

Similar to my beginning in San Francisco I attracted a good following of students early on. I was teaching dance technique through improvisation and running a long term (three months) performance workshop. Several months later student interest in my work dwindled and I had run out of ideas of where to take the technique. People with dance experience weren't being challenged enough while non-dancers did not like the constraints of the exercises. The one thing I didn't understand was why wasn't I worried?

After ten months in Australia, with my temporary visa about to run out, Lynden and I went back to the United States to get married. Neither of us wanted this. We both had an aversion to the concept of people being legally bound to each other. To us the commitment to the relationship was more important than commitment to a commitment. However, the only way I could receive permanent resident status was to marry an Australian and so I did. Twenty-three years later we are still married and this year, for the first time, remembered and celebrated our anniversary.

Returning from the States with my permanent visa in hand, we moved into a converted factory building, 97 George Street, Fitzroy. The building was owned by a good friend, Zandie Acton. It was she who brought Terry Sendgraff out to teach trapeze dancing in Australia and this was the space Terry taught in. Zandie had converted the two storey building into a combination live-in dance studio. It was great being able to live and teach in the same space. I even turned a small room into a woodworking space to make Hum Drums. What a boon not to have to travel to work.

I had first met Zandie in the United States. She had come to the University of Minneapolis with Bob Beswick back in 1972. Zandie, an Australian, had been studying with Alwin Nikolais. She decided to follow me to San Francisco, staying for several years after marrying an American by the name of Joe Dolce of 'Shaddupa Your Face' fame. It was Zandie moving back to Australia that precipitated me meeting Lynden, which in turn led to my move to Australia, and looking even further back it was Bob Beswick who precipitated my meeting Zandie. I continue to be intrigued by how a small incident in a friend's life can eventually lead to a major influence on your own life. Zandie accompanying Bob to Minneapolis was the first link to me meeting my wife and moving to Australia. Zandie met Joe Dolce through a woman who was doing classes with me in Berkeley California. How different our four lives would be if Zandie had not travelled to Minneapolis with Bob.

It was in the George Street Studio that I found the key to my style of teaching. I believe it was the format of the class rather than its content that initially proved valuable to myself and the students. I decided to give up the idea of teaching dance technique through improvisation and totally focus on improvisation as a performing art. Two things seemed particularly important to me. One was the need to perform frequently in front of an audience. The other, to make sure the development of students' personal styles became the main thrust of my classes.

Instead of three-month long workshops I taught short term (one-month long) performance workshops, having an informal performance at the end of each month. In order to study with me, students had to commit themselves to one four-hour class a week, plus an informal performance at the end of the month. They paid for the full series of classes and as part of the package would get a one-on-one session with me. The one-on-one situation was something I so thoroughly enjoyed and valued as a student of belly dancing in Berkeley that I incorporated it into my own class format.

This workshop package proved to be a big hit. The first two weeks, which often saw a fresh face or two join the classes, had the atmosphere of starting something new, a getting-to-know-you kind of excitement. The last two weeks had the adrenalin rush of a fast-approaching performance evening. The private sessions assisted students to work on and develop their own style of self-presentation, and performing in a very informal atmosphere each month did away with a lot of the performing anxiety that stifles improvised performances. Even though they may be frightened by the thought of putting themselves in the spotlight, people do like to perform. The basic philosophy behind *Theatre of the Ordinary* is that performing is for everyone and not just the professionals. This concept helped alleviate the fear of performing and also played a major role in the development of a student body.

The people who came to see their friends perform experienced a relaxed, warm and inviting environment. Finger foods and hot drinks were on offer both before and after the performing. The improvised nature of the performances, the mix of movement and language, and the varying quality of the presentations created a feeling of communion between audience and performers. More than that: the performances were very accessible and non-intimidating so that friends of the performers would think, 'I could do that', and would join their friend in the next workshop.

My first month long performance workshop had three participants, Bob Thornycroft - had had one professional boxing match, before he became a modern dancer – a young teenage woman Ellen, and my wife, Lynden Nicholls. It was such a great success that all three returned the next month. There were no new members but everyone was enjoying the work, especially me. The third month saw the student population grow to five people. Numbers continued to increase and by the end of the year I was teaching two workshops a week. Some great students started doing the classes regularly. Andrew Morrish, Peter Trotman, Helen Campell, and Rinske Ginsberg joined Lynden to add energy and talent to the workshop. These people became the early professional performing group known as Theatre of the Ordinary.

As well as the professionals there was a good group of non-professionals who kept coming throughout the year. Micheala Hellier, Jeanette Young, David Mackay, David Brier and John Sinclair became regulars, staying for over three years each. Then there was Robert Reid who was a very special case.

When Robert did his first series of classes I thought here is a total non-talent. His awkward jerky movement and stumbling speech was the book cover that I judged, or I should say misjudged him terribly by. It took a couple of years but Robert found his voice, the words and the characters that made him one of the most

consistently good performers in my class. He was the essence of Theatre of the Ordinary, a place where ordinary people achieve extraordinary results when they find their own personal style of improvised theatre.

The nature of my teaching by now was undergoing a complete change. By eliminating the concept of teaching dance technique through improvisation I was forced to evolve scores that dealt more with theatrical devices. I had to look at what performing elements combined to enliven a performance. My decision at that time to deal only with the solo form of improvisation helped me to isolate some important fundamentals. By naming and understanding these I could start building a knowledge base that would aid each person to develop their unique style of improvised performance.

'Positive Feedback' was the most important element to emerge. Essentially, I believed that always giving positive feedback would help give people the confidence to approach their improvised performances with gusto. It not only helped to alleviate negative judgement, it also became a very powerful learning tool. The *Eye to Eye* chapter of this book covers in detail the various values inherent in this form of analysing a performance. My reasoning for incorporating it in my practice came from the time I was doing Gestalt therapy.

Terry Sendgraff advised me to join one of the groups led by Anita Feder, a Gestalt therapist working in Berkeley, California. Terry had been involved in this work for a few years and felt very strongly that my joining a group would help our relationship. She wanted me to be able to express feelings more easily. So eventually I did join a group and continued going for several years. It was a very important step. The first thing I said in the group when asked what I wanted to get out of these sessions was, 'I want to learn how to talk'. And over the years of therapy that did happen.

I would watch with growing amusement as time after time a pattern would emerge. A woman who was unsatisfied with the man she was in a relationship with would join the group. She would verbally beat up, scream at, kick and generally abuse a pillow, the substitute for her partner. Gestalt therapy involves the client acting out various scenarios, usually a past incident. All of us in the group would get behind the woman as she vented her anger on the pillow, the villainous boyfriend getting what he deserved. The energy in the room would become very electric as a sense of reality emerged from the psychodrama. After a few months the woman would leave the group and, fairly soon after, her by now ex-partner would join the group. He in turn would re-live his version of the relationship, venting his anger on the pillow representing her. And we would all support him as he was able, to communicate his feelings about the relationship. This is a very simplified overview of Anita's group work but the important thing was that she set up an environment that allowed people to feel safe in expressing extreme emotions. The communication of these was the important factor. The factual truth of a situation, who was right or wrong, was less important than the free-flowing energy of communication.

I wanted to re-create this same energy flow in my classes. It was very important that students got rid of the self-critic who inhibits the flow of movements and words. The evaluation of good, bad, right and wrong was to be replaced with a different atmosphere, one of impulsively doing whatever you wanted in order to find the things you really enjoy. Hence positive feedback became the device that accomplished this aim.

Just as the uninhibited outpouring of emotions in therapy is only the initial step in learning how to express feelings and communicate clearly, so impulsive behaviour in itself was not the end point for me but the very important beginning of the development of improvised performance. The scores I devised combined elements of doing anything you wanted but within parameters that helped students develop many theatrical skills. I would use a few carefully chosen words to present the parameters students were to work within, what I didn't say was of equal importance to what I did say. An example of this kind of score would be: *Make and break physical contact with your partner, giving the breaking of the contact more importance than the making of it.*

All the scores I was developing involved either movement or vocal sounding, or were designed to help people find their theatrical use of language. I deal with most of these in detail further on in the book but I'll present a selection here to give you an idea of what I was exploring in my new teaching pedagogy.

PHYSICAL SCORES

ISOLATED AND GROSS MOVING: Shifting between isolated (moving one or two body parts while the rest are still) and gross (moving the whole body at once) movement.

IN PLACE, STILL AND LOCOMOTION: Being clear about whether you are staying in place while you move, being absolutely still, or travelling through space.

INTERNAL, PERIPHERAL, AND EXTERNAL SPACE: Where is your attention? Is it on the inside of your body, the surface of your skin, or outside yourself?

THE STEP WITHIN THE WALK: An exploration of what your foot does when it leaves the floor, what it does as it travels through the air and how your foot re-contacts the floor.

INITIATOR/RESPONDER ROLE-PLAY: An aid to develop movement vocabulary. This is done with a partner. Each person takes a turn being responsible for creating movement and responding to movement.

VOCAL SOUND SCORES

ASPIRANT SOUNDS: Exploring sounds that use only the breath, no vocal chords allowed. Whistling is discouraged in this score since it is a musical rather than an air sound. Play with shaping the lips and mouth to help vary the texture of the sound.

LIP AND MOUTH PERCUSSION: Exploring as many different ways the lips, tongue, gums and epiglottis can create percussive sounds without using vocal chords.

Phil Lip (sic) Mitchell

VOCAL SOUNDING: Any sound that uses the vocal chords.

I have students work with these ways of producing sounds, first isolating the three possibilities then combining them.

LANGUAGE SCORES

FAST TALKING: A timed two minutes of continuous and slightly faster-than-normal speaking. This is designed to eliminate the self-critic. By adding alliteration (the repetition of the same letter sound, "s" sound or "b" sound or "p" sound etc) to this score a student will be developing their ability to choose interesting words while speaking.

ONE WORD SENTENCES: Saying only one word, giving it the feeling of a full sentence. I also have students vary the length of pauses between words.

GIBBERISH: Sometimes called 'gobbledygook', it is the use of sounds that sound like but do not constitute a real language. Helps students expand their emotional range when speaking.

BEGIN WITH A WHISPER: If you want to go from movement to language but no words present themselves begin with whispering gibberish. Let the whispered gibberish gradually change to real words and then increase to normal speaking volume.

THE PRONOUN GAME: Start off with just speaking pronouns; you, me, us, we, them, he, she, etc., until your mind unconsciously starts adding other words to fill out a sentence and develop the text from there.

My one-to-one sessions gradually became a wonderful source of new concepts for me to play with during my regular class time. The process I used in facilitating participants' individual development in their solo sessions was to describe what patterns I saw in their improvisations, I would then create a score that helped them to feel, understand and further enhance what they were already doing. Here are two examples of one-to-one scores that I used for students whose main form of communication was through speaking to the audience:

Student A, let's call him, was what I perceived to be a wandering storyteller. He would walk aimlessly around the space as he created and told stories to the audience. Walking was an important element for him since, as he said, it helped him to think about and generate the elements of his emerging narrative. The score I created for him was to walk at times in a specific pattern, such as towards and away from the audience, or parallel to them, and also sometimes to continue with his aimless wandering. I also offered the possibility of slightly speeding up and slowing down the rate of his pacing, even stopping for just a moment or two so he could feel the distance between the audience and himself.

Student B's pattern was to alternate between doing some abstract movement and speaking to the audience. Whenever he shifted into speaking he would always stand close to the audience and address them directly. I had him explore talking from various parts of the room, and as well as addressing the audience directly he could also project his speaking out to the universe.

A similar result occurred in both cases. The voice quality while speaking had more expressive variation. The distance from the audience dramatically affected the performers and coloured their use of language, because this factor causes variation in emotional content – usually vulnerable when close, more secure when further away. When working one to one with students on this concept I use the term 'felt distance' hoping this will instil in them recognition of the emotional effect distance has between audience and performer.

A basic concept I now play with all the time came directly from doing these particular one-to-ones. It's my *Who Are You Talking To?* score. I offer the possibility of four entities the performer can communicate to: themselves, a real or imaginary partner in the performing space, the audience, or the universe. It doesn't matter what the form of communication is. It can be

47

movement, sound, song or word. The important aspect is the intent, who or what is being engaged with. By recognising these possibilities and learning to shift between them, an emotional reality seems to envelop the performer and this will be felt and enjoyed by an audience.

As with teaching, my method of directing improvised performances, and of performing, changed. In structured improvisations several elements are usually pre-defined. These include order of events; specific use of props; and music that is preselected for specific moments. Actual movements and/or words are improvised. Instead of this approach, I decided to opt for performance that was totally improvised, where the only thing known is how long it would last. I was not performing solo at the

David Wells   Gll Shaw   Al Wunder   Lynden Nicholls   Lynne Santos   Andrew Morrish

time. I had formed, and directed, the performing arm of *Theatre of the Ordinary,* initially made up of Lynden Nicholls, Peter Trotman, Andrew Morrish and myself. About half a year later Rinske Ginsberg and Gill Shaw joined us and another year later David Wells and Lynne Santos became part of the group.

I wanted the performances of Theatre of the Ordinary, or TOTO for short, to combine the elements of anarchy and democracy. We rehearsed twice a week under my direction, which included having each person facilitate sessions from time to time. The group aesthetic that I wanted to achieve was performances where our individual stories and personalities emerged. As a group we worked a lot on how to support a solo, how to take a solo, to give a solo, to be left with a solo, to fight for a solo, to relinquish a solo, to let a solo emerge slowly. We allowed for lots of entrances and exits. There was a music corner where we played musical instruments or did vocal sounding to support what was happening in the middle of the performing space.

We performed many times at various venues around Melbourne. The only thing we knew about each performance was that it would last one hour. A radio alarm clock, which we set at the beginning of the show, would start blaring out some song or news item sixty minutes later, signalling to us and the audience that the show had come to a end. We gave our shows names such as: *Not Just Your Ordinary Crocodile Attack, Hedgehog SlicLamenting the Moose, Grotesque under Stress.* They were titles without relevance since we never knew what the content of our shows would be.

There are various ways you can contextualise a totally improvised program for an audience. For example, I wrote some program notes about us for the time we performed in the Adelaide Fringe Festival. I used a comic yet somewhat truthful approach for describing our personalities since it was the mixture of our personalities that became the material for our improvisations. The soap opera descriptions gave the sense of knowing and empathising with the characters.

LYNDEN NICHOLLS: Comes from a good family background. She's humorous and articulate both in movement and language. An organiser who makes sure everyone is at the right time in the right place and thinks anyone crossing the street when it says 'DON'T WALK' is naughty.

GILL SHAW: Tough, strong willed, political. She's the school marm you never wanted but always appreciated afterwards. Gymnast, juggler, clown. But don't let her fool you, she's a softy underneath.

PETER TROTMAN: Figgin's famous computer whiz kid. Upwardly mobile in his dancing and his lifestyle. This young man could barely afford $200 shirts while on the dole two years ago. He'll bowl you over with the power of his voice and beauty of his imagery, all seven stone of him.

AL WUNDER: Mr. Universe not in body, but in the way he thinks. He seeks ultimate truths with his Zen spirit. A penguin freak who can be awkward and graceful at any one time. He's quite deaf but this doesn't stop him from singing out of tune or speaking out of context.

ANDREW MORRISH: Nice guy. Warm hearted and a good mixer. He's witty and full of fun. His satire however will cut at all social conventions. Beware the sharp velvet tongue.

DAVID WELLS: The awkward grace of the untrained athlete abounds in this man. He's an animal lover who moves to unheard rhythms. He's fearless and will try anything once, twice if he's still alive.

LYNNE SANTOS: She's the dark one. Dark hair, dark eyes, dark moods. A beautiful mover who can make you laugh or cry as she comes to grips with life and its relationships.

All in all we performed and taught in a variety of different environments. At one point we realised that six out of the eight of us were working independently in the disabled community. So we pooled our resources and applied for and received several grants that enabled us to take our form of theatre into this circle.

In 1987 after being together for four years the performing entity that was 'Theatre of the Ordinary' amicably split up. David Wells and Lynne Santos formed 'Born in a Taxi' with several other people. Andrew and Peter began their wonderful collaboration as 'Trotman & Moorish'. Lynden and I did some duet performing for a while. Gill Shaw moved to Darwin and Rinske collaborated with various performing artists in Melbourne. I kept the name Theatre of the Ordinary, however, and have continued to use it ever since as it defines so well the philosophy at the heart of my work.

Two years earlier I was forced to move from George Street because the building was being sold. There was a one year hiatus in a scout hall in West Brunswick. This was the only studio I have taught in that I totally disliked.   It was dark and cold and perpetually dirty.   At the end of that first year I noticed a newspaper add of a studio for hire at 112 Cubitt Street, Richmond.

Cubitt Street was to be my home for the next thirteen years. After a couple of weeks, however, I almost walked out. The advertised 3000 square feet of clear space turned out to be only 1600 square feet. A quarter of that was taken up by the various paraphernalia being used in the teaching of arts and crafts to intellectually disabled adults. The 'clean' floors were embellished by a few years of accumulated dust. I had paid for a month's use of this 'gorgeous large clean studio' and could not back out because I needed a place to teach. But I vowed to leave as soon as I could.

When I entered the room for my third week of teaching I

saw that all the tables being used for the craft activities had been removed. I closed my eyes and visualised a sanded, polished Jarrah floor, red wooden beams elegantly supporting a wood-panelled ceiling, exposed red brick walls with high windows running the length of the east and west walls, twenty-two 150 watt floodlights with gel frames and various coloured gels to light the performing area, portable seating which would comfortably seat fifty to sixty people. When I opened my eyes one month later there it was. The home of Theatre of the Ordinary, 112 Cubitt Street Richmond, Victoria.

It wasn't magic. It was easy. The old Jarrah floor needed sanding, the walls cleaning, a few power points added. The lights I had already made from donated electrical materials two years before. The room already had everything else. There was even a small room I could use as an office down a small flight of stairs. I signed a year's lease with the Uniting Church, the owner. Now I had my own space to teach in whenever I wanted, and to rent out to other interested teachers and performers who also needed studio space. I was in business. Cubitt Street would prove to be a beautiful warm studio where many people would explore and develop their craft.

By now improvisation as a performing art had begun to flourish. Teaching continued to be my first love with on-stage activities playing second fiddle to the educator. The development of the work depended on the energy and quality of the students who passed through the studio. Many worked consistently with me for five years or more. By 1997 I had initiated a new type of class. I called it the Extended Performance Workshop. It was, and still is, designed around ten weeks of classes, incorporating two six-hour long sessions per week. It was a bridge that I built for those students who wanted to explore a more professional and extended style of performing than they were able to evolve in my regular workshops, based as these are on two to five minute performances. The aim is to develop an ability to totally improvise a thirty minute performance. Each extended workshop culminates in two weekends of public performances, allowing the participants to express and showcase the extension of their improvising skills in both solo and duet work.

Four companies were now performing regularly and becoming very popular. Nick Papas, Penny Baron, Brenda Waite Lynne Santos and David Wells were the founding members of Born in a Taxi. This is a group that creates wonderful physical theatre. They are visually beautiful with a great flair for costumes.

Group improvisations are extremely difficult because an unplanned agreement must be clearly acknowledged by all members of the troupe while the show is actually in progress. Their ability to shift from abstract to character and present an improvised sixty minutes of theatre that looks well scripted and rehearsed is amazing. They are equally well versed in improvising text or doing a whole show with just movement.

The strength of the duet performances of Andrew Morrish and Peter Trotman was their ability to combine verbal game play and witty monologues with some very unusual movement sequences. There was the classic straight man (Peter) with a long thin body and the comic (Andrew) smaller and a bit rounder. This physical difference added a visual humour to their very funny improvised text.

Claire Bartholowmew, Michael Hurwood, Andrew Gray, Jarod Benson and Sandra Pascuzzi formed the group 'Five Square Meters'. Developing characters and situations is the style of this group. Gestures, postures, movements and words help to convey the sticky situations they create for each other. The humorous way they try to extricate their characters from these fabricated situations is the essence of this quintet.

Janice Florence and Wendy Smith joined forces with

Martin Hughes, Jacob Lehrer and David Corbett to create 'State of Flux'. They are five people developing a form of contact improvisation that includes elements of theatre and non-contact dance. Janice is a wheelie who has been paralysed from the waist down for several years, making the company a multi-abled one.

These groups that developed an audience and gave improvisation the professional status it still has in Melbourne today. David Wells, Nick Papas and Andrew Moorish are also three of the four members of the Urban Dream Capsule. They won the award for best theatre event in the 1996 Melbourne Festival, living and performing for fifteen days in Myer's Bourke Street Store windows. Since that time they have spread their wonderful improvising performing skills, taking the Dream Capsule to Hong Kong, London, Paris, Brussels, New Zealand, Chicago and beyond, eating, sleeping, bathing, talking, writing and performing in shop windows twenty-four hours a day for anywhere between fourteen to eighteen days at a time. They are the ultimate improvisers, spreading the joys of improvisation internationally.

Though I myself was not involved in this development of

professional performance I continually organised many performing events in the studio. Closest to my heart were the ongoing student performances. I had changed the duration of my workshop program from four to five week blocks, mostly to fit in with the ten-week school terms. Many of my students were parents, as I now was, and this was more convenient and manageable. Every five weeks there was an informal performance given by the students of my three classes. We alternated between 'In House' performance, where the only audience was those who were doing my classes, and 'Out House' performance where we invited friends along. It worked out that there are four in house and seven out house performances each year. I still follow this format.

It was in these 'House' events that a whole range of styles emerged. There would be anywhere between ten and thirty people performing five-minute solos and duets. Some of the performers would have only attended five classes with me and had never performed previously. There were others who had been doing my classes for many years. Several of the performers would have had dance or theatre training from other teachers. The variety and varying quality of the performances made for a delightful mix of funny, serious, powerful and tentative vignettes of improvised theatre. After several years at Cubitt Street I felt the need to organise performance evenings that were more professionally oriented. The improvising skill level of several students demanded something more challenging than informal performances. I also wanted to bring together the diverse music, dance and theatrical improvisers from around Melbourne and instigate more intermingling between the performing arts.

This led in 1990 to my organising an event for the Melbourne Fringe Festival called *Spontaneous Generation*. There were three weekends (Thursday - Sunday) of improvised music, dance and theatre. My brief was to bring together dancers, actors and musicians who used improvisation as their primary form and mix these various media together in an evening's presentation. ach night's program had at least one dance, one music and one acting event. Several of those taking part intentionally mixed these elements together to create multi-faceted performances.

Spontaneous Generation lasted for four years, 1990 –1994. It was not a great financial success but artistically it brought together the diverse improvisational talents of many Melbourne

performers. Having Warren Burt organise the music side of this Festival deepened my working relationship with him. I also met and chose to involve myself in various performances with musicians Robert Jackson, Carolyn Connors, and Simone De Haan so it was a particularly enriching time all

Al Wunder and Simone De Haan round.

The other big performing event that I launched at Cubitt Street was *A Year of Fridays*. As the name suggests there was a performance given every Friday night for a year. We started on the 29th of May 1996 and finished on the 30th of May 1997. This idea was happily plagiarised, with her consent, from Terry Sendgraff. In the early eighties she ran *A Year of Sundays*, in which she herself performed every week for a year. Most of her performances were solos with a few duets and group pieces.

A *Year of Fridays* was designed to give various performers and groups an ongoing event in which to showcase their developing talents. Unlike *Spontaneous Generation* this turned out to be both a commercial and artistic success. There was an average weekly audience of thirty to thirty-five for the year, culminating in two hundred people cramming themselves into Cubitt Street for the closing night. Thirty-five of them were performers, the other one hundred and seventy made up the audience, a very gala event indeed.

———————

Cubitt Street had become the performing centre for improvisation in Melbourne. There would have been at least twenty weekends of performances every year. For me it was the place where the teacher in me began to understand what I was teaching and the positive effect it was having on many people. It was in this space that my teaching of three, four and even five classes a week clarified, solidified and further developed my teaching concepts. It was there that I began writing this book.

The 12th of December 1999 was *Grand Final Day*. This was the name I gave to my last day in the Cubitt Street Studio. The Uniting Church had sold the building and we had to move out. I organised a gala event, inviting all my past and present students to participate in one last performance. It took over five hours for all the performers to strut their stuff. It was a very sad and happy occasion. Students I hadn't seen for years came and honoured the space with their presence and their performances. Putting the padlock on the gate for the last time, I cried for the loss of something I loved dearly.

27 NOVEMBER 1999

A couple of weeks ago Wendy Smith asked me to write a 300 word article for Proximity Magazine. It was to be about the final days of the Cubitt Street Studio. That evening thanks to Wendy something beautiful happened. I realized I had fallen in love again, this time with a studio.

You didn't sleep well last night? No I didn't!! Were you crying? Yes!! Why? Because I am going to be leaving you soon. But I'm just a room. No you're not!! Not any more!! You were once, thirteen years ago when I first arrived and cleaned your floors an hour before our first class together. You were just a room then. Hey, maybe you spruced me up a bit, sanded my floor, added some pretty lights, fixed some windows, but really all I am is an empty space surrounded by bricks, mortar and wood. No you've become something much greater than that. To begin with, you have the most beautiful voice. No matter who is talking you make them sound good. Then there are your eyes that let in the sunlight, casting moving sun shapes on the soft red colour of your floor. Your walls and ceiling also dressed in red, create a warmth that is so rare to find in a studio space. And that is just the physical attributes that you possess. There is a spirit in you now that is so much more than the red-coloured clothes you wear, the exquisite texture of your voice and the magic of your eyes. It is the spirit of hundreds of people who have danced, sung and spoken their thoughts and feelings about their lives, their loves and their fears. Don't you think you are being a bit melodramatic here? I mean I am totally made of dead material. There are no recording devices embedded in my walls. I am just a space, nothing more. You will take with you when you move the spirit that you just spoke about and put it in another space. A month ago I would have agreed with you. But each time I leave your presence now I take the time to look at you and see something that is alive and vibrant. Something with a unique personality, which in essence, in my emotionally-filled eyes at the moment, makes you a "someone". I will miss you.

You didn't sleep well either last night? I never sleep!! Were you crying? I don't know. What were you doing? Memorising the stories of Sandra, Anna, Carolyn and Jillian. I thought you said that you were not alive. I wasn't before you wrote this but I am now. I will miss you too. Thanks for giving me a life.[3]

---

[3] An article written by Al Wunder for the magazine *Proximity* Volume 1 Edition 4 December 1998

5

MOTION IS MY LANGUAGE

If a picture is worth a thousand words, how many words are contained in a movement? How many verbs, nouns and adjectives does it take to convey an equivalent amount of information inherent in the moving body? For me the language of motion has a different reason for existence than that of the spoken word. It is the physical sensations of movement or the emotional sensations brought on by movement that are so attractive to me. I delight in lifting and lowering my arm at different speeds or at different angles to my torso, at varying my posture while walking just to see how this will affect the use of my legs. I love experimenting physically because of the different sensations this type of play brings about. It is only in recent years that I have realised it is the emotional as well as the kinaesthetic shifts a finely articulated movement brings to my awareness which makes dance a more important means of communication for me than words.

Though English was my first language motion became my language of choice. Being able to communicate through movement was why I became so turned on to improvising within an abstract dance structure. With my first improvisation I suddenly found a way of speaking that was easy for me.

I've already touched on my difficulties with verbal communication but two episodes as a teenager really illustrate my lack of fluency and ease. One wasn't a single event but an ongoing occurrence with my father during my teens. When I turned thirteen I started working in my father's machine shop during summer vacations. He had a very small business that manufactured and repaired soda-bottling machinery. The staff was made up of my father, a full time machinist and a part time bookkeeper. I worked during school holidays doing regular 8 AM to 5 PM shifts, five days a week.

We lived about an hour's drive from the workshop. So two months a year for five years my father and I would drive to work, in silence. We so rarely spoke to each other. It wasn't from lack of love or respect but what I assumed to be two shy people being in a confined space together. I would try to think of how to initiate conversation but just couldn't find anything worthwhile to say. Most likely it was the generation gap and a particular male pattern of only being able to talk with your workmates. I didn't have too much trouble talking to my friends and my father would always be involved in animated shoptalk with his business associates whenever I noticed them together. I never knew if my father was as uncomfortable about this situation as I was.

The second event occurred when I was seventeen. I asked a young woman if she would go to the movies with me. We were friends at school and there was a good movie showing in the city. It was a 30 minute bus ride to the train, a 45 minute train ride to Manhattan, a 2 hour movie, the train and bus ride back to her house plus the waiting time for public transit vehicles to arrive. I couldn't think of a word to say, nor obviously could she. Total embarrassment wouldn't adequately describe my feelings of that evening. I was afraid there was something wrong with me and that I'd never be able to carry on a normal conversation. This became a great concern of mine during my late teens.

I believe it was the combination of shyness, a genetic hearing loss and the long times of isolation with broken legs that contributed to this feeling of social inadequacy. When I started to improvise with Nikolais' abstract dance scores my shyness disappeared. The communication was visual instead of aural. I found a whole new language that I could easily converse in. Motion became my language even though I had no idea of what I was saying.

For the past few years I have kept peeling back the layers: why was abstract dance such a powerful force in my life? Why did I drop out of university to pursue something that seemed to have no meaning? A career that offered no monetary return to a lame dancer didn't seem the most logical of choices to make. However, it wasn't in my nature to deal with practicalities and I had an overwhelming need to connect to, converse with, and communicate through movement instead of words. But why? What was it about movement, about abstract dance that caused me to make the right choice about what to do with the rest of my life?

One answer that seems to fit was the therapeutic value in being able to express the buried feelings of the physical and emotional trauma resulting from the succession of fractured femurs and the long periods of loneliness that followed. I remember my early solo improvs having short, sharp, angular, erratic movements often ending in a crouched or prone position along the back wall of the room. I remember feeling pleased, sad and excited all at the same time.

Once, while giving feedback to a student, I had an insight that proved valuable in deepening my understanding of my love of the abstract. I stated that abstract movement was the language of emotion and words the language of content. With words we describe the who, what, where, and when of an event. Body language and facial contortions as well as texture of voice communicate emotional sub-text. Movement is the unspoken language that adds substance, credence and colour to our speech. This is what had so attracted me to abstract movement, its ability to enunciate and articulate emotions without words. Alwin Nikolais' teaching, with his distillation of dance choreography into the abstract elements of time, shape, space and motion, helped me to develop a physical language that I treasure to this day. My ongoing work has been to dissect these four elements even further and create an immense reservoir of movement vocabulary that would help remove the belief that dance is only about agility and grace. My class structure reflects this philosophy, offering people a way to connect with and enjoy a multitude of shared movement experiences with others in order to develop a physical language that is just as understandable, varied and moving as a verbal one.

My sister-in-law says I am loose with my use of language, which is quite true but there happens to be a purpose to my seemingly slack play with words. Take the terminology I use to describe one of my classes, 'Motional Improvisation'. The word "motional" does not exist but it more accurately describes what I do than 'dance improvisation'. 'Movement improvisation' is grammatically and descriptively correct but 'motional improvisation' seems to imply something deeper and more exciting. Interestingly, no one, not even my sister-in-law has mentioned that motional is not in the dictionary.

I have also changed some of the more common terminology used in dance classes since I no longer consider myself a teacher of dance. I do this as a means of challenging students' perceptions of what is expected of them. Most dance classes begin with warm-up exercises, the loosening up, stretching and strengthening of muscles through set routines. I have replaced the word 'warm-up' with 'personal physical play' wanting students to be personally responsible and creative in the way they stretch, strengthen and prepare their bodies for physical exertion. I want them to make their own decisions about how they wish to develop as physical beings through exploring various options. I want them to find the connection of mind/body/spirit through experiencing how their choice of physical play affects their way of being in the world.

I still have moments when I feel guilty ignoring my early dance training as I lead my students through personal physical play. To assuage my conscience I offer the names of dance teachers I respect to those students who wish to develop specifically the technical dance skills of flexibility, strength and balance. What I teach is the other half of technique, a strong awareness of the body in motion and a clear articulation of movement to the point that it becomes a language. It is in this part of my class where students build the motional vocabulary which colours how they physically converse with other students.

I do not do any teaching in the first ten minutes of my class. Students are told that this is their time to work however they want to prepare themselves for improvising. It is the time where they learn the process of bringing themselves into the present. The concept of presence and being present is vitally important for an improviser. The ability to focus on what is happening rather than what has or what will happen is one of the more important skills of improvisation. It sounds so easy but just try standing alone in the middle of your living room and extemporaneously creating a ten-minute soliloquy that has some meaning. Now imagine appearing in front of an audience of fifty or more people and, without any pre-planning, creating a thirty-minute theatre piece. The improvising performer must have the confidence and skill to begin with any movement, sound or word knowing that they can then develop it into a cohesive performance. They need to hear, see and feel the internal and external stimulus of each moment in order to react in a theatrically viable way. Each person must find his or her own device for achieving this ability to be in the moment. These first ten minutes when I am not teaching is the only time students can practise the skills of decision making, being present and being involved without stimulation from an outside source.

I don't demand but suggest this, however, and unfortunately it is the rare student who actually arrives early enough to put these first ten minutes to good use. Most arrive on the hour and by the time they are changed there is only a minute or two left before I start teaching. Others spend the time chatting with a friend waiting for 'the teacher' to give them instructions. I do not remonstrate with those who are late but periodically reiterate the value of using this undirected time of class wisely. This non-authoritative approach is part of my process in breaking down the hierarchical relationship between student and teacher. I am only there to supply information not discipline. Students must take responsibility for their own learning, which to me means they are allowed the choice of being on time or being late to classes.

When I do start talking, ten minutes after class begins, I take students on a trip through the body, calling out the body parts I want them to focus on as the primary movers, the place where movement begins. Some defining parameters such as lifting and lowering the primary mover towards and away from the floor focuses a student's attention, yet still leaves room for limitless explorations. The trip is designed to give students the experience of moving in response to a variety of physical sources. I, for example, have always been an arm and hand person. These are very strong sources of creative movement for me. Left to my own devices most of my movements would unconsciously emanate from this area of my body. By having to deal with various parts of the torso and legs as primary movers I will increase my patterns of physical behaviour and find new ways of moving thereby enhancing my motional vocabulary.

As I take students on a trip through the body I ask them to be aware of some choices they have unconsciously made, indicators of habitual patterns they established many years ago. These are their choices of verticality, place in space, and balance between physical skills and creative play. Verticality is the decision to work standing up, lying down, kneeling or sitting on the floor. Place in space involves whether one stays in one spot in the room or includes travelling as part of the exploration. The balance between physical skills and creative play is the time spent deliberately working on flexibility, strength, speed and balance in relation to the time spent just enjoying movement for its own sake. I call attention to the options of changing their verticality as much or as little as they want, staying in place for the whole half-hour or moving through space as part of their practise. I also ask them to be mindful of their balance between physical skill and creative play, which can be fifty/fifty, a hundred/zero or anything in between.

By calling attention to these three aspects of movement, which we tend to take for granted, I introduce the idea of multiple awareness and multiple choice making. I want students to look at their patterns of behaviour in relation to verticality, locomotion and creative play and take responsibility in each class for restructuring what they do to fit their physical and emotional needs of that day. I am hoping that students will change the way they involve themselves in personal physical play. For example, someone who habitually does most of the personal physical play lying on the floor and stretching his legs might also begin to include some standing creative play, using the upper torso, arms and head. And conversely someone who tends just to dance rhythmically to the music will begin working on flexibility and strength.

My scores are designed to offer students a huge range of movement possibilities to play with, incorporating the use of various body parts as primary movers, and exploring different sizes, speeds and textures of movements. Students can then choose to spend personal physical play time developing further those movement skills that interest them the most. In essence the students take responsibility for developing their own technique.

Here are two of my favourite personal physical play scores, one with a single primary mover the other with two. I tend to use single primary movers as a way of differentiating how we move from certain parts of the body and multiple primary movers as a means of integrating movement throughout the whole body. By using a single primary mover students expand their awareness of the different movement patterns that occur when using feet or hands or hip or legs as the initiator of the dance. To some extent we all have a body part or two that we tend to lead with, parts that seem to stimulate us creatively. As stated previously for me it has always been my arms and hands. Conversely there would be a few body parts that we hardly ever use as primary movers. My torso is the laziest of my body parts and I continually practice using it as a primary mover in order to wake it up.

Focusing on two or more primary movers at the same time can be a great help in integrating the moving parts of the body. Think of dance or motion as a physical language that requires the clarity of enunciation and articulation similar to that of a spoken language. It is the intricate coordination of lips, tongue, vocal cords, jaw and soft palate in our mouths that produces multi-layered sounds into patterns of speech. Similarly the coordination of arms, legs, torso, head, fingers and vision etc. helps to enunciate the physical words a dancer uses.

What follows is a re-creation of the way I present this material so that you can get a feeling of what actually happens in class.

JOINT MOVEMENTS

(Recorded music is being played throughout the personal physical play, including the first ten minutes when I am not speaking. The students are already moving as I begin speaking and they continue moving as I take them on a trip through the body.)

65

Let's start with the joints of your fingers as primary movers. There are two types of activities you can do with these joints. One is the actual physical manipulation of the joint, bending, straightening or rotating the joint. The other is the movement of the joint through space.

(I throw in the following clarification after a few minutes)

Try isolating these activities, working the joints without moving them through space or move them through space while the joints themselves are still. Now specifically combine those activities.

(a few minutes later)

Change your primary mover from fingers to wrist joints, isolating and combining the physical manipulation of the joints while moving the joints through space...how much or how little of the rest of your body are you allowing to move with your wrists.

(a few minutes later)

Continue your explorations with the elbows as primary movers...check into your choice-making about verticality, place in space and the balance between physical skill and creative play work.

(Giving a few minutes to explore movements with each body part, I continue the trip through the body, shoulders, spine, hip, knee, ankle, toe and face joints being primary movers).

MOTION TO STILLNESS RELATIONSHIP

You have the top of your spine and the bottom of your spine. Sometimes move the top of the spine while holding the bottom gently still...sometimes move the bottom while holding the top gently still...sometimes move the top and bottom of the spine together and when you do be aware of whether they are moving in the same direction or in different directions. As you work with the spine also maintain an awareness of your choice of verticality, place in space and balance between physical skill and creative play work...how much or how little are you allowing the rest of the body to move with your spine.

(I let students work for several minutes before I speak again)

Now using your right and left shoulder as primary movers sometimes move one shoulder while holding the other gently still, sometimes move both together, paying attention to whether they are moving in the same or different directions.

(after another several minutes of working with the shoulders)

Switch your attention to your knees, sometimes moving one while letting the other be gently still, sometimes moving both together either in the same or different directions.

(several minutes later)

Now deal with your hands and feet, which means you have four different primary movers. Which ones are being still and which are in motion? Explore the various possibilities of stillness to motion with these four body parts, including the possibility of all four moving together either in the same or different directions.

If you haven't already done so become aware of your vision. When do you work with your eyes closed, when do you work with them open. If they're open are you seeing what you're looking at? If they are closed what are you seeing/feeling?

In very general terms there are three possible things that you can see with your eyes open, your own body (arms, legs, hands etc.), your environment (walls, ceiling, floor, objects in the room) or people within your environment. See if you can find a natural way to shift your vision from one to the other.

(After several minutes I have students work in pairs and the partnering phase of class begins.)

Some other things I enjoy doing while taking a trip through the body is dealing with three qualities of movement, vibrations, undulations and extensions. This score offers a range of speed variation to the expansion-contraction activity of muscles. Vibrations require quick alterations between expansion and contraction. Undulations are a sequential extension and release of muscles along a specific length of various body parts. Extensions are long slow movements in one direction.

Several times during the year I use non body-part oriented scores as a change of pace. I once began my class with what I called the Fred and Ginger exercise. Without hamming it up, working on their own without a partner, students were to emulate the grace and elegance of Fred Astaire and Ginger Rodgers lightly moving through space to some beautiful ballroom dance music. Exploring forwards, backward and sideways locomotion, pausing, turning and every once in a while redirecting someone's pathway by putting an arm around the back of their shoulders and taking them with you. A delightful score that had the wonderful quality of surreptitiously working on several areas at the same time, coordinating use of leg joints to promote graceful movement, spatial awareness in order not to bump into anyone while travelling backwards and sideways, as well as aerobic endurance.

Wrestling? Yes, I've done that also. It certainly creates a quality of motion that is not often seen in dance classes. Using any part of the body students at first gently and then not so gently pull and push each other which becomes a wonderfully playful strengthening exercise. I used this score in a class with all women

and they truly loved it, getting totally into the extreme physicality of mock aggression, which comes with pulling and pushing using all your strength without an objective of winning a contest. They were laughing, grunting, rolling on the floor, totally exhausted after several minutes of this activity. The feedback that followed was extremely animated, the energy in the room sky high for the rest of the class.

My wife Lynden's Feldenkrais training has influenced my thinking about personal physical play a great deal. In particular it has instilled confidence into the evolution of my work on differentiating and combining the use of various body parts as a movement source. I semi-plagiarised one session she did with me which involved moving my head sideways and then back to centre.

In the next day's class, I asked the participants to move various body parts towards and away from a centre rest position, starting with the head. Then to explore a variety of distances their movements would take them from their centre. We also dealt with pathways that went in straight lines and pathways with curves and what results when equal attention is given to returning to a centre rest position as is given to the moving away from it. A sensitivity to the totality of a movement ensued. Normally we are most interested in the end of a movement rarely paying attention to how the movement began and how it progresses to its end point.

As one becomes more attuned to the minutiae of motion both the internal and external pathways can be felt. Let's say you are reaching for a glass of water. One possible external pathway would show your hand leaving its centre rest position from your side and reaching in a slightly circular motion to the glass. The hypothetical internal pathway might be this: if you are sitting your hip will tilt slightly forward, sending a small ripple up your spine and moving the shoulder three millimetres to the front diagonal as the upper arm lifts and straightens the elbow; this in turn causes the wrist to bend minutely inwards before extending outwards with the fingers straightening and then bending in order to encircle the glass. Just be thankful we don't have to say it before we do it!I have described how I vary my use of basic parameters such as body part differentiation; direction of movement; the physicality of joints and muscles; qualities of motion; and opening and closing the space between parts of ourselves (hands to feet…). My reason for these variations is to find new ways to sensitise students to their own movements. I rarely repeat the scores that guide students in their personal physical play but invent variations to basic themes that get them to pay attention to their physical sensations (hopefully pleasurable) as they move their bodies in a variety of ways.

———————

SIX DEGREES OF AGREEMENT

The second section of class focuses on working with partners to guided scores, which continue to foster greater enunciation and articulation of movement. Now, however, we are dealing with a conversation between two people. This partnering section is extremely valuable for two reasons. Firstly there is a natural growth of motional vocabulary that occurs as students share their physical  patterns of movement. Secondly with a dialogue of motion occurring rather than a monologue the need for establishing an

 understanding and coming to an agreement creates the search for a common language. The participants in the duet need to find a reason for their being together. This might be the enjoyment of a similar movement experience (rolling and balancing on knees) or the recognition of being involved in the same situation (looking towards and away from each other).

The clarity and articulation of movements during the process of initiation and response helps duet partners find what in general terms is called "the game". In order to achieve this it is necessary to evolve a language of theatre and movement understood by all participants. Language is the means we have of connecting with each other and interaction is the means of developing language. You really can't have one without the other therefore, just the act of working with a partner automatically creates the atmosphere of finding common ground.

In fact, many more than six levels of agreement must be reached before an understandable relationship occurs. As part of the continuous investigation into the options possible in creating exciting communication without words, I introduce a series of "articulators". These are the basic articulators, the necessary articulators and an endless supply of clarifying articulators. For the basic articulators I have taken the concept of movement and divided it into three categories, which define all the possible ways of moving: *in place*, *still* and *locomotion* movements. I define *in place* movement as moving as much as you want as long as you don't travel anywhere. *Still movement* means being absolutely still, and *locomotion* is the act of travelling from one place to another. My aim in creating this differentiation is to give students a simple focus, a commonality of observation, one degree of agreement that they then can relate to each other with. It is the simplest breakdown one can do with movement. We use these three elements of non-verbal communication constantly, even in our everyday lives. Take the situation of being out somewhere with a friend: invariably when one person walks (locomotion) the other will follow suit. If one stops and looks in a shop window more than likely so will the other. Being absolutely still is rarely done when we are not sleeping with possibly the exceptions of daydreaming or meditation. People who are involved in a relationship however more often than not sleep together thereby sharing long periods of stillness with each other.

The previous examples depict a relationship of similarity within the basic articulators. This does not always have to be the case. I hate waiting on a street corner waiting for the "DON'T WALK" sign to change to "WALK". My wife feels it is important to follow these directions. So often when we are together in the city I will cross the street (locomotion) as soon as I feel it is safe to do so while Lynden waits for the "WALK" sign to appear (stillness). I would then wait on the other side of the crossing (stillness) until she catches up (locomotion). At first we had a bit of an argument (in place) of the rights and wrongs of jaywalking before continuing on our journey (locomotion). Now we just accept our differences and there is much less tension as we move out of and back to similarity of in place, still and locomotion with each other.

The necessary articulators, the initiating and responding to each other, is something done unconsciously all the time when we are with someone. We shift between initiating and responding when speaking to other people. We are constantly communicating, finding agreement or disagreement about what we want to do or not do with whomever we are with at the moment. "Life is an Improv", as Ruth Zaporah once said during an improvised performance. In fact the only place we find it difficult to improvise is in the performing arena. In our regular day to day life we do it all the time.

When not performing we naturally interact (improvise) with internal and external stimuli but onstage we live in a different reality. The difference is that the improvising performer must communicate to an audience whose reason for being there is to be entertained in some way. I believe it is the fear of not being interesting enough that makes improvising in front of an audience so troublesome. In order to maintain their interest, theatre must live in a more compact time than reality. Performers need to present a story which moves from beginning to end at a speed much faster than the story would have taken in real life. In other words one of the major skills needed to create a theatrical event is the ability to aesthetically condense our stories to fit into an hour or two of real time. It is this skill of condensing real time to theatrical time which must be learned before a performer can be comfortable improvising in front of an audience.

Though the time sense is different the true essence of improvising, spontaneously reacting to the combination of internal and external stimuli, is the same theatrically as it is in reality. Whether in the performing space or everyday life, we interact by initiating and responding to each other. I often include initiator and responder role-play in my scores, with one student as the designated initiator to the other's responder. They stay in these roles until I say "change".

Primarily I do this to strengthen students' ability in both roles. My personality, for example, tends towards responding rather than initiating. My wife on the other hand is definitely an initiator and our conversations often begin with her talking first, enthusiastically and at greater length than my short-sentence replies. Our conversations are most interesting, however, when I am willing to talk with equal gusto, generously putting forth my ideas as well as responding to hers.

When two improvising performers are really firing, the roles of initiator and responder become indistinguishable. It is important however to distinguish these roles in the classroom so students can recognise the power inherent in each one. By introducing scores that define the terms initiator and responder and how they differ from each other students increase their ability to find and develop a movement conversation.

The task of the initiator is to show the responder a movement and observe what the response is. By observing the response, the initiator's following movements will of course be coloured by this. Conversely, since the responder can respond in any way (as long as it is a direct response) to what the initiator does, the responder becomes equally responsible for finding and developing a physical conversation. Unlike verbal conversation where one person talks at a time, in a movement conversation both dancers will tend to move continuously. This tends to blur the edges of who is initiating and who is responding.

The responder has the option of responding with varying degrees of similarity. I use the following terminology to describe some possible layers of similarity and difference. *Yes/yes, yes/and, yes/but* and *no way*. *Yes/yes* is total agreement: 'I really like what you're doing and will do exactly the same'. *Yes/and* is almost complete agreement but with an additional element to be dealt with: 'Yeah, I really like what you're doing, I'll do the same thing and how about adding this variation to the equation'. *Yes/but* is a partial agreement but with a desire to do things differently: 'Okay, I'll run around the room with you but I'll do a different type of run. *No way* is total disagreement (agreeing to disagree): 'No, I am not going to do what you're doing, I want to do my own thing. If you continue standing like a statue I'll run towards, away from and around you'. There is dramatic potential inherent in presenting these optional responses in this way but I also clarify for my students that one can enjoy doing very similar or very different movements together.

I find all of these relationships theatrically viable, each having an emotional dynamic that can vary between pleasing, irritating and humorous. Our everyday need for companionship sees almost all relationships fall into the *yes/and* type. The *yes/yes* and *no way* are the least seen, either in the classroom or during performances. I imagine this is due to the clichéd look of the *yes/yes* which most people try to avoid because they think it is very boring to watch. The *no way* mode is quite an uncomfortable relationship to deal with even in theatrical terms because of our natural desire to make a connection when we are with someone. Fortuitously, my wife was taking photos when a wonderful example of when a no way relationship presented itself in a workshop I was teaching in New Zealand. Steve Hollins set himself on top of a pile of gym mats where he busied himself with some inconsequential hand gestures. Wah (that's his real name) was into a wandering locomotion, aimlessly traversing the room muttering inaudible words. Just that scenario was quite funny and then, well turn the page to see what happened.

Two, three, four or more people doing the same movement at the same time impart a visual beauty to the movement simply by the weight of numbers. One can also find interest in the unusual combination of several different body shapes. The dynamic tension between characters that are not in agreement with each other can put an exciting edge to a performance.

The *yes/but* relationship is one of struggle, epitomised in the endeavours of two people who want to find agreement but have yet to agree about how to agree. If both parties acknowledge and agree to continue working in this state it can become quite a humorous dialogue of movement and/or words.

A variation to the designated initiator/responder score is to have students choose and change their role anytime they wish so that at times there will be two initiators or two responders, as well as times when one is initiating while the other is responding. This highlights the fact that there may appear to be very little difference between initiating and responding yet the distinction is a necessary element of interaction between people.

THE CLARIFYING ARTICULATORS

There are countless elements that go into making one moment of theatre. It is impossible for any individual to pay attention to more than a few of these at any one time. So we do classes to learn what we need to learn and then practice certain elements to the point where they become a skill. A skill is something we develop through conscious repetition of an act until we can do it automatically without conscious effort. Several factors come into play in determining to what degree we develop our skill in various areas. These include our personal choice of those things that interest us, our potential in those areas, the willingness to apply ourselves to developing a higher degree of skill level as well as the opportunity to do so. Unless we are born with some physical disability one of the earliest skills we acquire is that of speaking. The skill of communicating through speech requires developing the ability to automatically combine several elements that make up the phenomenon we call language. Enunciation, developing vocabulary, creating meaningful sentences, connecting sentences in order to clarify our ideas, modulating pitch and volume to give emotional context to our verbal statements, are just some of the components necessary for carrying on a conversation.

We learn the rudiments of language by an early age and, by the time we are five years old, can communicate quite well with others. The next several years of schooling advances our skill level to varying degrees, depending on each individual's desire to learn the nuances taught to us. People who choose occupations such as politics, public speaking, writing, acting, do even more training to enhance their language skills. This development is necessary to succeed as a professional. In every stage of development an individual's interest and desire to improve determines the level of articulation reached.

The term 'articulators' actually describes what I teach in my classes. My scores are all designed to get students to be more articulate in a specific element of theatre. Just presenting the concepts of the basic and necessary articulators helps pupils create more cohesive and vibrant improvisations. Further development of an improvisation occurs as several clarifying articulators are used along with the basic and necessary ones. There is always a host of clarifying articulators present in any improvisation. It is the recognition of the potential communication value of a particular clarifier that adds another layer to performance.

Teaching improvisation as a performing art creates something of a conundrum. The most exciting elements of improvisation are contained in its sense of freedom and expecting the unexpected. Yet form and structure are necessary ingredients for a performance. My method of dealing with this paradox is to present scores that have little if any limitations on what students can do physically but which at the same time create a single element for them to focus on in order to learn something from the experience.

I create scores that isolate various aspects that occur within movement theatre. This helps to give students insights into how they might combine several elements in order to create a good performance. These elements are the vocabulary and grammar that bring fullness to the voice of the theatre, something that can be developed and enhanced through awareness and practice. You'll find in the appendix, 'A Score of Scores', a list of scores on various topics, including exercises on the basic articulators, necessary articulator and the clarifying articulators.

My current teachings have evolved from further distillation of the four basic building blocks, *TIME, SHAPE, SPACE AND MOTION,* which I learned from Nikolais. These are present in every performance. It is the director's job to mould these various elements into a successful theatre piece. All I ask of my students is that they become their own directors. Oh yes, they must also be choreographer, writer, actor, and dancer. Some even add the skills of the composer and musician to their performer's kit bag.

As improvisers we become the Jacks-and-Jills-of-all-trades in the performing arts. Needless to say my teaching has to cover a large body of work. The combination of teaching privately in my own studio and working with multi-level instead of beginner, intermediate and advanced classes, has fostered a style of pedagogy that is accumulative rather than progressive. New students can join my classes at any time without feeling that they have missed something. Students who have been with me for years find themselves presented with either new material or variations on old scores. No one knows, myself included, what topic will be covered on any given day. The students learn from each other through the process of observing and emulating what is important or interesting to them personally. Experienced students unconsciously teach by example, they themselves becoming simpler and more precise when they work with newcomers. Repetition of concepts occurs frequently but with variations and in different combinations with other ideas. This non-linear method of learning in a mixed level environment seems a natural form of gathering knowledge and is similar to the way we learn language as toddlers.

Time. Shape. Space. Motion. Like the game of chess you can spend a lifetime creating theatre pieces by varying the possibilities inherent in these four building blocks of choreography. The dynamic flow of a performance can be enhanced by judiciously highlighting one or the other of them. Being well versed in the use of all four is a tremendous aid to the performing improviser. As a student's skill level in the use of time, shape, space and motion rises by working on specifically designed scores the aesthetic use of these elements becomes semi-conscious or even unconscious. What I call 'a base level of goodness' develops, supplying the improviser with an artistic form to support impulsive play. Many of the scores I use now are derived from these four elements. The following is a list of how I initially sub-divided time, shape, space and motion in order to explore nuances within each of the topics.

TIME: **Time as speed** (how fast, how slow): The most obvious use of time is speed. Speed of movement creates a certain energy both in the doer and the watcher. Changing and varying speed opens up the possibility of developing a dynamic structure, which can be shaped to suit the emotional needs of the moment.

Time as duration (how long):   How long do we stay at a certain speed? How long does it take to change from one speed to another? How long do we maintain what we are doing? Duration and change are ways of sustaining and varying moods. It is also an important part of the illusive and highly valued skill called timing, classically used to describe the good comedian, 'she has a great sense of comic timing'. Performers can develop a feel for how long to hold a pause before the punch line or just when to grace the audience with a meaningful glance.

Qualities of time (rhythmic, erratic, sustained): Rhythmic time is movement to a regular pulse or beat. Erratic time consists of sudden changes of speed and a lack of specific pulse or beat. Sustained time is continuous movement that neither speeds up nor slows down. I have also had students play with unusual time definitions such as crazy time, my time, no time, sad time, thinking time, and so on, purely as a means of exploring time from an image or emotional base. Some people find creative expression more easily through images while others work better with using physical reality as a departure point for exploration.

SPACE: **Physical space**: Where am I? Am I indoors or outside? If indoors, how close am I to each of the walls in the room? If outside, am I near a rock or a tree? Where is the audience? How close am I to them? Am I alone in the performing space?

If not, how many other people are there and how close am I to them? How you are placed in the performing environment makes an important statement to yourself, to anyone you're performing with, and to the audience.

The most important aspect of physical space is distance from the audience. The visual and emotional impact of a performer who stands very close to the audience is quite different from standing a long distance away. Similarly, but to a slightly less extent, the distance of the performer from the periphery or centre of the performance space also adds an emotional context to the story being told.

The term 'space shaping' is used to describe the effect one or more bodies in space have on an audience. Acknowledging the proximity between performers and audience is one of many articulators which help to clarify the emotional/visual communication of the moment. Students learn what emotional timbres various areas in the performing space have for them through working in solo mode to the score of, *'be aware of the distances between yourself and the peripheries of the room'*.

As well as spacings, students work with the relationship of facings as part of their vocabulary. Facings describe the front to front, back to back, back to front, side to side relationships between performers. As a performer one should also be aware of which view the audience has of you, and how you are affected when you present your front, back, side, or diagonal aspect to the audience.

Personal space: Personal space deals with how far performers extend their energy to the outside world. I look at three possible ways people can deal with their own spatial energies: internal space, peripheral space and the external space. When performers are involved with internal space they are paying attention to what is going on underneath the skin. They are less aware of what is going on in the outside world. Their own thoughts, feelings and movements outweigh the need to overtly communicate to the external world.

Peripheral space: Concentrates awareness on or close to the surface of the skin. By focusing directly on their own physicality, performers call attention to the shape and movement of the body itself. It is as if the performer is saying to the audience 'look at my hand as I move it up and around my head. Continue watching as I open the space between my arms'.

External space: Is an extension of energy outside the self. Now performers can initiate visual connections with other performers, the audience and the environment they are performing in. This has the potential to enliven all of the space in which the performance is taking place. The audience's attention is now being directed beyond the performer to the environment of the performance space and any other performer in that space.

By exploring and shifting between these three aspects of personal space, performers create a more interesting interpersonal dynamics with the audience. They can direct energy out towards the audience and then slowly pull the audience's energy towards themselves by withdrawing into a personal space. This is a very natural occurrence. You can observe it the next time you are in conversation with someone. Notice how the person talking to you shifts from the internal (eyes focused inward looking thoughtful as they form the words and context of their statements) to the external (looking directly at you as they reach the conclusion of what they are saying).

SHAPE: What kind of shape are you making right now? Are you sitting or standing? Is your back straight, curved, twisted? Do you have your hands at your side or are you reaching for something? Are you sitting in a full lotus yoga position, standing on your head, or doing an elegant ballet arabesque? Our bodies are always making some kind of shape. Sensing the communication value of whatever shape we are in imbues that shape with dramatic significance. If we can feel comfortable with simply standing and looking at something while being watched by an audience then for that moment this is all that is necessary. As the moment passes our shape must of necessity change, whether this is just a facial shift or a subtle postural variation. This is so because we are alive and teeming with emotions. I attended a workshop taught by Margaret H'Doubler (1889 – 1982) in the mid 1970's where she defined the word emotion as, "*e* (the need to) *motion* (to move)". She is often thought of as the mother of dance education in the American University system. Her first creative movement class began at the University of Wisconsin in 1917.

When I was dancing with Nikolais shape was a very important element of our choreography, as it was and still is today with many contemporary dance companies. The strength and flexibility of the trained dancer's body can create more spectacular looking shapes than the untrained body. Extraordinary flexibility is one attribute I do not have. My flexibility would be considered quite ordinary, which in the Australian vernacular means very poor. The flexible dancer can bend and straighten limbs in the most unusually complex manner.

In my early dance training I would watch in awe as some of the more loose limbed students spent time in front of a mirror looking for and finding a beautiful and seemingly impossible shape with which to begin their dance. I was quite envious at the time but my physical limitations soon had me finding a choreographic style

 that was less abstract than the dances created by other students. My more humanistic and theatrical shapes were quite unique in Nikolais' classes and suited not only my body but my aesthetics as well. Simple shapes which can be achieved without dance training are just as valuable in communicating an emotional story, as long as performers feel and value the shape they are making. I now look upon shapes as falling into the categories of pedestrian, distorted and spectacular.

MOTION: For years I never really understood or felt motion as a source of creativity. As far as I was concerned motion was synonymous with dance. Dance was motion and any type of motion was dance. Early in my developmental work in Berkeley, I defined dance as 'a specific shape, moving at a specific speed, through a specific space'. This definition seemed to cover every type of motion until I witnessed a performance in 2002 by Weave (a multi-abled troupe), which changed the way I thought about motion. I don't know why it took me so long to perceive and value this particular element for its own sake but suddenly the various shaking and undulating movements in the choreography overrode my predilection to see everything in terms of time, shape and space.

As I thought about what I had seen I recalled that Nikolais often spoke about 'kinetic motion' and I began to envision the possibility of dividing motion into two categories, kinetic and contextual. Movements such as shaking, vibrating, undulating, twisting and rolling suddenly seemed to have a vibrant continuity about them. This had the effect of diminishing my hitherto emphasis on shape, time and space.

David Wells, one of the members of Born in a Taxi, quite often includes what I now call kinetic trills to his locomotion. He will add to his rhythmic walking an undulation, or a bobbing up and down, or just a movement of the head from side to side. The repetitious movements add a humorous motional quality to what is an already delightful character.

Many years have passed since I first began extrapolating various ideas from the precepts taught by my mentor, Alwin Nikolais. Though my teachings now have little resemblance to what I learned from him I still use the concept of breaking things down into three or four smaller blocks which can be explored separately before being reunited into a gestalt. This process of breaking down and rebuilding is most evident in my 'Extended Performance Workshop' a special series of classes I teach every year. In this workshop I work with what I call 'The Four Modes'. The Four Modes are Pedestrian, Character, Caricature and Abstract, names I have given to some basic ways performers have of presenting themselves to an audience. In the extended workshop I first have students explore and develop each of these modes separately and then work with combinations of these modes as a means of modulating the dynamics of the performance. Dissecting performance practice into different modes helps to hone specific skills such as the ability to develop a character or using abstract movement as a means of creating a mood. Learning how to integrate the various modes helps the student develop a longer and more interesting performance.

What has become evident to me through my teaching these many years is that our movements whether they are done on stage or in real life communicate so much more than we think they do. Motion is a shared language. We each have a distinct way of moving. Our postures clarify whether we are happy or sad, angry or in love, open to receiving companionship or wishing to be alone. Movement can also help change the mood we are in. Dancing to music with friends is a very uplifting enjoyable experience. Competitive sport (if not taken too seriously) can be emotional as well as physically valuable. The ever shifting moods of playing well one moment and poorly the next, jumping for joy when a goal is scored, make us feel more alive and excited. Physical play is extremely important for our well-being.

So play sports, go for a walk, a swim, ride a bike, or have a fun-filled wrestle with a friend or lover. We have all done these things at some time in our lives. Hopefully most of us are still doing at least some of them. I am, but even more importantly I still engage in abstract movement play (dance) two or three times a week, thoroughly enjoying having long physical conversations with people, talks which are devoid of words but full of communication. I do this because motion is my language.

6
THE FOUR MODES
PERFORMING....... *a person forming*

In 1997 I began teaching an extended performance workshop. Meeting twice a week for ten weeks, each class lasts six hours. The work is designed to prepare students for performing thirty minute solos and duets. The emphasis of the class work switches from physical articulation and developing confidence in being impulsive to elongating themes that emerge from the beginning of an improvisation. Two topics, *the four modes* and *the en game* as I call them, are explored as a means of helping students to recognize and develop a sense of structure to the improvised performance.

Our way of being in the performing space has many faces. There is our own face (pedestrian), the faces of Romeo and Juliet (character), the face of the harlequin (caricature), and the face of the dancer (abstract). These are the four modes. As improvisers, we must decide who we are at the beginning of our improvisations. Who we become depends on what is most theatrically appropriate for each moment of performance. No matter how we choose to disguise it what we present to the audience is in reality a self-presentation.

Self-presentation: a provocative concept you might think when used in the context of theatrical performance. It smacks of self-indulgence and audiences supposedly abhor the self-reflective actor. They expect to see an actor play a part, be a character whose reality is the figment of a writer's imagination. But is not this figment a self-presentation of the author, a communication of his or her life experiences through the social, moral and political viewpoints of a character?

Whether playing Good Samaritan or Devil's Advocate the dramatist asks and answers ethical questions important to him or her. And with the actor not really being responsible for a character's actions audiences will accept any carefree, benevolent, evil, ugly or self-serving behaviour as a theatrical device. What is true for the playwright is true also for the composer and the choreographer. Each of these is presenting aspects of themselves through the intermediary of the actor, the musician, or the dancer.

Improvisers, whether acting, dancing or singing, become both the creator and the performer of their own work. The immediacy of improvisation demands that performers must present some semblance of self that is meaningful to them and which they wish to share with an audience.

So here I am, the improvising performer, entering the performance space, supposedly without any preconception of what I am going to do; what should I say or do that will start me on my journey of spontaneously generating a theatre piece? I must make a choice and more and more choices as the improvisation unravels, but on what do I base my decisions?

A simple answer is past experiences: what I have seen as an audience member and found most enjoyable, and what I have done as a student that has enriched me, that feels aesthetically valuable and allows me to communicate clearly what I want to say and how I want to say it.

If I were a purist I would choose just one of the performing arts — music, dance or theatre — to create my performance. However, I am not a purist but rather a jack of all trades so I can sing, dance or act my way into beginning a performance, shifting my mode of presentation anytime I wish. There is yet another important choice to be made. How do I sing? How do I act? How do I dance? Will I be myself or a character, or a caricature, or just a shape in space? My thoughts whirl through the myriad of choices at my disposal. You would think after so many years of improvising that I could quell pre-performance mind-chatter. Since this seems to be impossible I have learned to enjoy these mental improvisations by not taking them seriously. Experience has taught me that all preconceived ideas disappear as soon as I start.

Tonight I raise my arms and silently begin dancing. What a relief! The mind games are over and I am in the real time of improvisation, unconsciously using the skills I have developed for over thirty years, instinctively moving from one step to another, from one moment to another, from one performance mode to another.

The following definitions of pedestrian, character, caricature and abstract offer a guide to the understanding and exercising the four modes of being as a performer. There is no fine line dividing the first three but a hazy grey area exists between pedestrian and character and between character and caricature. If you draw a long, longbow you might also find a grey area between caricature and abstract. We all have our favourite performance mode, our home base. Evolving some basic skill levels in the other modes will expand one's theatrical vocabulary.

PEDESTRIAN
I think I think. Therefore I think I am, I think. (sic)

If you were watching a particular exercise in one of my classes some years ago you would have thought the pedestrian was a sad, lost soul with caved in chest, stooped with age, dragging weary feet in slow shuffling steps, in other words carrying the weight of the world on his or her shoulders. Never mind that the people doing the exercise were in their mid-twenties, vibrantly healthy and for the most part extremely athletic. I had instructed them to be their pedestrian selves and walk around the room as if they were walking down the street. The transformation was immediate. Everyone aged fifty years and became the pedestrian as described above. I have found the same phenomenon occurring in many classes over the years when I've asked people to perform just being themselves.

It is not often one finds an individual who, without verbal prompting, views their pedestrian self as a happy, energetic, open and vital human being. Most of us live with the misconception that our everyday lives are less interesting than those of characters in plays, movies or novels. This is absolutely not true. So why, when asked to perform being one's self in front of an audience, do we downgrade our energy and become the uninterested and uninteresting pedestrian. Perhaps it's because we live in a  society that has developed a prodigious sense of paranoia about strangers to the extent that we create psychic barriers around us, not looking at others for fear that, 'What the hell are you looking at buddy?' might be the response. Or we might be afraid of frightening someone with our uninvited interest. Let's call this the newspaper syndrome, keeping one's vision from extending beyond the arms-length necessary for reading newsprint. It is this syndrome, this disinterested, introverted character, which most people present when asked to be their pedestrian selves in the performing space.

To circumvent this response I now introduce the *pedestrian performer* to students as the *enlivened pedestrian performer* in order to help them find and  project the entertainment value in their normal everyday lives. This is the self at its best, happy, and confident, on top of the world. There you are, out there, fearless, communicating openly, speaking to the audience about your life and beliefs in a very natural way. This is what Terry Sendgraff was so good at, being interesting simply by being herself. She could be walking down the street, dancing at a party, talking to you in a coffee shop or performing solo in front of a large audience. For her it didn't matter whether she was happy or sad: whether she was content with herself or going through the trauma of a radical mastectomy because of breast cancer. Her need and power to communicate feelings of the moment, eliciting neither sympathy nor advice, was what made her the perfect performer of the pedestrian mode.

A few others who have studied with me also fall into the category of natural pedestrian performers. One who immediately comes to mind is Jenny Bigelow. Jenny was very different in personality from Terry. She was darker, more contemplative, with a very pessimistic view of world politics. Caught in the dilemma of wanting to help those who were snared in powerless situations — the poor, the homeless, the abused — her stories and musings evolved around her inability to help them. Her work was always thought-provoking and challenging. It gave rise to thoughts of how to change certain apathetic attitudes within society, getting audiences to look at ways to be more politically vigilant and active.

On several occasions she used a ladder to climb up to the rafters of the studio from which she gave vent to her anger on the mythical 'powers that be'. She opened doorways into the real world that existed beyond the make-believe world of the performance studio. I mean this literally. One doorway of a studio where I taught opened onto a fairly messy back yard while another looked out on a street scene of cars and pedestrian traffic. During one improvisation Jenny opened the doors to these vistas and moved in and out of the studio and the real world, dramatically emphasising her desire to change the world into a better place.

Her final performance as a student remains one of the most memorable improvisations I have witnessed. Jenny was the victim of an accidental infant bath-scalding and was left with some horrific scarring of her torso and arms. Her choice of clothing for the evening was a short sheet which half-covered half-revealed her body. The more she moved the more she revealed. Self-exposure was her intention.

I can't describe the language used, twelve years have passed since then. The performance revealed pain, trauma, love, happiness, and moral dilemma. Soap opera material. Yet it was anything but banal. It was gut-wrenching, humorous, the life-affirming journey of a young woman who was real, fully alive, and creating one hell of a brilliant piece of theatre.

My father was in the audience with me that night. He had come from the United States to visit his grandson, my son, who was born three months previously. As I watched Jenny's body and life flash before my eyes I couldn't help but be concerned about what my conservative (this evaluation is mine not his) seventy-five year old father would think of what his son's work was producing. With trepidation I asked him if he had enjoyed the evening. His reply was "I really liked the last performance. (Jenny's) It was something very special."

In writing about Jenny and her work as an improviser I now realise that although her actual mode of presentation was always the pedestrian her best work used some fairly extraordinary theatrical set-ups — the ladder, the open doorways and the semi-nudity — as means of enhancing the entertainment value of her monologues.

I don't remember Terry ever using anything other than herself and her life as a means of entertaining when she was in her pedestrian mode. The last time I saw her perform was during *A Year of Fridays*. This was a year-long series, from May 1997 to May 1998, consisting of a performance every Friday night in the now defunct Cubitt Street Studio in Richmond. I plagiarised the concept from a similar event that Terry ran in Berkeley California in the mid 1970's. She called hers *A Year of Sundays*. The plagiarism was done with Terry's full knowledge and consent and helped entice her to visit me here in Australia. She couldn't resist being the star attraction for a night in an event that honoured her and her groundbreaking work as a performer.

The first fifteen minutes of performance was Terry at her pedestrian best. She stood up in front of eighty strangers and spoke about her plane flight across the Pacific. She explained and demonstrated the various methods she used to try and stretch out a sore hip muscle in the cramped economy section. This was her method of creating a warm light-hearted atmosphere that involved the audience in her life. After that fifteen-minute monologue she could do no wrong, the large majority of people had fallen in love with her for an evening.

The different personalities of Terry and Jenny demonstrate vividly that there are various ways of presenting one's self in the pedestrian mode, and that a variety of personality traits will emerge if performers are true to themselves and their emotional make-up of the moment. With practice students come to realise that like any character in a play they have emotional highs and lows, and to allow the natural flow of emotions to inform them and their audience of the dramatic tensions and comic relief inherent in living a life.

Performing in the pedestrian mode expands one's theatrical vocabulary by offering a means of down-shifting dynamic energy. Both audience and performer perceive a slowing  down and softening of the environment. The pedestrian performer creates a relaxed living room atmosphere by addressing the audience in a simple matter-of-fact way, becoming a friend to those watching. Some in the audience seem to want to join in the conversation. Some actually do, and there have been times where a dialogue between audience members and the performer becomes the developing material. For the most part, however, the performer is left to create a monologue, which is very often autobiographical.

To me there is very little difference between someone's personal history and a fictitious character's. Each one of us has been exposed to an extensive range of emotional experiences through various events in our lives and therefore our stories are just as valuable for an audience as those of Captain Bligh or Hamlet. By exploring one's own past and present life for source material to develop an improvisation, the student soon realizes that the more personal one becomes the more universal the themes that emerge. Audiences relate their own personal tragedies and triumphs to those that are presented to them by performers on stage.

Each of the modes has its particular way of being on stage and its value as an exercise in the classroom. There are also the grey areas that exist between pedestrian and character, character and caricature, caricature and abstract; the zones in which things can shift and mutate. As a performer I often experience those times when I am right on the edge of being a character or being myself in pedestrian mode, unable to define clearly for myself which of these two I inhabit. So I am willing to accept and work

with this definition of blur, both as teacher and performer, as a valid concept in its own right.

CHARACTER

All the world's a stage and all it's people potential characters

There are six billion characters living on this earth right now, four billion more than have died since Homo Sapiens first appeared on this planet. Contemplate this statistic: two thirds of all the people ever born are still living. It seems quite unbelievable. Yet I heard it on ABC radio, the science show with Robin Williams. Imagine trying to calculate how many characters have been brought to life on stage and in manuscripts since the human race began writing and performing for each other. Some of these characters never really die, they keep being reborn. Take for instance Romeo and Juliet who are over four hundred years old. Their story has been told thousands and thousands of times. Many of us in the west will know about their families, and the motives and interrelationships that led to their tragic deaths.

These two famous lovers are an example of the traditional convention of scripted characters who arrive on stage with personal histories and personalities. Such characters also come complete with a script, which is then played out in dramatic or comedic form. Improvising performers, however, do not have the luxury of knowing the background of an emerging character during performance. They have to deal with a different entity, what I call the implied character. This is a fictitious person whose actions and reactions are governed by the physical and emotional feelings of the improviser as these arise and are expressed during performance. There is no history of a set character with known characteristics to call upon. The birth of this parentless and placeless being with no name and without script can come from one of three sources: movement, imagery or voice.

Movement by itself can often evoke an emotional reaction in the performer. This evocation of mood and the ensuing movements which follow produce for the audience a suggestion of character especially if the mood is reflected in the face of the dancer. I'll use myself as an example here since the abstract has been such a strong element of my performance style. The changing of my body shape or varying speed and size of movements become the catalyst for a shifting of moods. The dynamic variations of mood affect my face as well as the rest of my body, helping to personify my movement and give the sense of character to my work. I become not quite myself. A hint of character appears, a hint of someone else inhabiting my body and reacting to the mood that is being generated by the movements I am making. I cannot describe this character other than that a feeling of loneliness and isolation often seems to be the predominant mood. I have learnt to stay with, heighten and change moods as a means of structuring the emotional flow of a performance piece.

Another way students have of creating character is through the use of imagery. Many picture themselves within an environment that determines the way they move. These mental pictures can take the form of an earthly landscape such as a forest or as in the case of Peter Trotman they can have an otherworldly quality about them. Peter, one of my very first students, alerted me to the fact that someone with an aptitude for abstract movement

might very well use imagery as the stimulus for exhibiting a sense of character while dancing. He is a very talented improviser who had a unique and beautiful style from the beginning. During an early one-on-one session I asked him what he was feeling or thinking while performing. He said he was moving within an imaginary environment and described moving through a world that had huge strands of spaghetti-like substances hanging from a deep blue sky. His movements depicted weaving and pushing aside the pasta-like substances while his face and vision created the reality of a character involved in the situation.

The third source of implied character can come from the use of one's voice while speaking or singing. It is very rare that students will use their own normal tone of voice when they begin talking in performance. More often than not an eight or nine year old characterized voice with corresponding physicality appears in students' early character-based improvs. I believe the young child emerges because people revert to the last time they

actually made up play characters, which tend to be in the eight to ten year old age range. This is not always the case but it is common in beginning students who have never participated in a drama course.

An exception to this theory is Brendon Murley. He has always been a strong speaker, working primarily in the pedestrian mode. Being a social worker he deals with families who are in difficulties and the early stories he told were often thoughtful and sad. His voice however tended to have a monotone quality to it so I created a score during a one-on-one session to help him enliven his pedestrian performer. I asked him to create a story about an archaeological dig and to change the texture of his voice three or four times during the telling. It was a huge breakthrough. To the surprise of us both a wonderful character emerged who spoke quite eloquently and with strong emotional expression in his voice. The improvised text was vibrant, humorous and compelling, the story an exciting mix of dedication, betrayal and murder. He had in effect moved from pedestrian to character mode. This added another string to Brendon's performance bow. He now uses character and caricature as predominant elements in his improvisations which have become much richer since that one-on-one.

Speaking with an accent is something most of us have done. Even changing the texture of our voice, giving it a rougher hue, higher pitch or more nasal quality transforms us from our pedestrian selves into a different person. Stereotypes such as the Jewish mother, the drunk, the snooty upper class Englishman or whiney three-year-old are created through the use of accent and voice texture. These stereotypes lend the implied character a sense of history. They don't need to have a name or known background for us to recognize them because they are part of our history, having seen them before either within our own circle of friends, or in literature, film, theatre, or television. These characters are easy and fun to play with. They are familiar to us and quite often we use them to elicit laughter from the audience, a means of gaining confidence in performance. They are a marvellous way of entertaining people.

Students who use character as their preferred mode of performance develop certain personality traits that frequently reappear in the characters they portray. As spontaneous inventions emanating from a heightened state of communication these implied characters can forthrightly express thoughts and feelings in ways we would not normally use in everyday behaviour. A case in point is the delightful Mr Sperm, who was brought to life by a long-standing student of mine, John Fenelon, while he was doing an extended performance workshop with me in 2001. Through several improvisations John was able to use this very funny and insightful character to express his excitement, fear and sexual yearnings at a time when he was trying to establish a relationship with a woman he had just met.

Mr. Sperm was a perfect character for John who is a very talented physical comedian drawing on a variety of techniques including gesture, posture and voice texture to create a personality. John is normally a shy and softly spoken individual. His character, Mr. Sperm, however was quite outspoken, gleefully pontificating on the joys of sex. It is a shame that his graphic description (physical and vocal) of Mr. Sperm's journey from penis to egg will never be repeated again.

The performing persona of the implied character is unique for each student, almost as unique as his or her own personality. Being an outgoing or shy person, having forceful, timid, lonely, happy or angry dispositions will possibly emerge as students further develop their use of character mode. With practice, students gain confidence in performing and the self-applied pressure of needing to use humour to entertain audiences becomes less important. As the students' work deepens their implied characters can assume the guise of more recognizable archetypes.

Archetypes such as the hero, villain, shaman, lost child, wise woman, fool or the hermit exist in every culture. They represent certain personality traits that can be found in all societies. We carry within us aspects of all the different archetypes. A few will predominate in each of us and form the basis of how we relate to the outside world. They also give rise to the theatrical style of the performer. The fool, the hermit and the wise man are the

archetypes that most dominate my performances. Through several years of work with me Noel Rees-Hatten has developed the archetype of the lost child to a very high level. The lost child is a natural extension of the soft voiced, inquisitive person that Noel is in her everyday life. The lost child appears in almost all of Noel's performances enabling her to poetically convey a story that easily shifts from being humorous to being profound. I used to think Noel should actually give her character a name and a costume to wear therefore making it a specific rather than implied character. The value of this would be the audience getting to know and feel this character as a real person. Each ongoing performance of this character would add a little bit more to her history and those of us who watch several performances would become interested in this fictitious person's life story.

Happily Noel did not go the way of the specific character but maintained the implied, and therefore more universal aspect of the archetype. By doing this, Noel allows audience members to more easily associate the archetype to their own lives. The specific character with a name and a history lives in a defined theatrical world that we can see into but are not really a part of. The implied archetypal character has neither name nor history and therefore creates a need in us, the audience, to fill in these gaps. We might see aspects of ourselves or someone we know in the personality of this character which allows us to become more emotionally involved with the performance.

An improvising performer never knows which character will emerge during a particular performance. It all depends on what he or she is feeling in the moment. If the improviser has planned nothing and has the confidence to allow their impulses to initially generate material then the minute variations of physical and vocal patterns are enough to give birth to a new theatrical being. You may not know the name of this fictitious person, nor his age, or her social and political beliefs, but the individual comes alive on stage, a person different from you who will say and do things you wouldn't say or do yourself. This is the joy of characterisation. It is amazing how forthcoming we can be with our speech and physical behaviour when we are cloaked in the guise of a character. We can go beyond our usual actions and let different aspects of ourselves to emerge thus broadening our emotional palette and physical vocabulary.

CARICATURE

caricature /karikatyooa/ noun 1A exaggeration of personal features or characteristics, often to a ludicrous or grotesque degree. B a representation , *esp* in literature or art, that makes use of such exaggeration for comic or satirical effect. [4]

[4] The New Penguin English Dictionary Penguin Books ltd. 2000

Freedom! The ham actor comes alive in this mode. The playful uninhibited child. Wilful! Taboos themselves become taboo. Outrageous! The editor and critic disappear. Any thing goes! Fantasies become reality. Silly and salacious! Social commentary dressed in satirical clothing. Witty wonderful words wafting without thought about their own self worth. Energy, high energy, extreme energy emerges and reawakens the slumbering innocent within us.

I have chosen the term caricature to differentiate a performing style that exaggerates the physical or vocal attributes of a human being, just as a cartoon caricaturist uses the device of enlarging certain facial or body characteristics to create a humorous drawing of someone. Most of us have seen performers portraying what I call caricatures at some time in our lives. The example that is most common to all of us can be found in the old silent movies. Early screen actors could not use the spoken word as a means of communication. This necessitated overly exaggerated movements and facial grimaces in order to explain the emotions and relationships between characters. This exaggeration gave these films their classic style of physical comedy and melodrama.

Back in the sixteenth century a form of theatre developed in Italy. Comedia Del Arte initially was named Comedia dell'arte all' improvviso' because of the improvised nature of their plays. They were performed entirely in what I call caricature mode. Players wore specially designed masks that "embody an archetypal emotional position and are stereotypical of a social class".[5] The interaction between these characters was so outrageously amoral that many people refused to attend performances while those that did found it hilariously funny. Lechery, cruelty and stupidity knew no bounds as the creatures that inhabited the stage went about their daily business of bashing and tongue lashing each other. The plays themselves were a series of bumblings, thumpings, and humpings. This was the origin of what we call slapstick comedy, which is the cornerstone for humour in silent movies.

---

[5] Rudin John & Crick Olly *Comedia dell'Atre a hand book for troupes* Routledge 2001 p167

One student of mine, Steve Hollins, performed exquisitely in caricature using a lot of Comedia del Arte elements in his improvisations. The ability to suddenly shift from the belligerent physically overbearing bully to a wimpy little victim was his forte. Physically and vocally he could so embody the caricature of each role that audience members laughed not just at his words and actions but at his expertise of quick shifting between victimiser and victim. Often he would find a delightful way of turning the table on the dominant bully as the wimp suddenly changed to being the top

dog. He would switch physically from high status (standing at full height and looking downwards) to low status (affecting a stooped posture looking up), while he maintained the original high and low pitched voice of each role. This created the extra challenge of sometimes having the wimpy high voice hovering in high physical status over the squatting gravely voiced low status figure. Would he be able to correctly connect voice to physical status as the changes came more and more quickly? He could most of the time, and that made the improvisation even funnier. But the real belly laugh came when he finally lost track of who he was when. His presence of mind and experience as an improvising performer allowed him to imbue his caricature with an exaggerated embarrassment that explained the mishap and therefore maintain the theatrical integrity of his performance.

As an exercise caricature mode offers untold riches. First of all there is the high energy output that comes forth from removing the censor in us. Physically over-exaggerating emotions such as anger, happiness, pain and remorse has this uncanny ability to free our verbal utterances to the point that they can become uncensored literary gems. Taboos are easily broken in this mode especially when given as an exercise from the teacher. When told to do something outrageous from an outside source we tend to feel less responsible for what emerges from following those directions and more willingly do and say things we would never do or say if left to our own devising. This willingness to let go of personal behaviour patterns increases the emotional range we are able to convey comfortably in front of an audience.

To help students who are reticent to let go of their normal everyday patterns of speech and physical behaviour I use the device of gibberish. This speaking in a made-up language offers

most students a playful way to involve themselves in character. When we remove the coherent value of words while carrying on a conversation with someone it fosters a more emotionally expressive use of hands, body, face and voice because movements and sounds have replaced words as a means of communication. Since most students have a lot of fun with this score it is quite easy to take the next step up to caricature which is the excessive use of physicality and voice texture. When using gibberish we free ourselves of the concern that our actual words will hurt someone or start a violent argument. This allows us to playfully get involved in hamming up shouting matches or melodramatic love scenes with other students.

The use of larger-than-life movements and speech patterns are not the only ways of performing caricature. Alicia Clarke is a student that uses words in such an outrageous way that I classify her favourite mode of performing as caricature. She is one of those rare people whose spoken language is a stronger creative source than movement.

Shocking and obscene images are a major element of Alicia's verbal content. She loves graphically describing the loss of any and all bodily fluids and has no qualms about depicting infanticide, matricide, fratricide or any type of murder and mayhem that you can possibly think of. She is a tall raven haired, open faced woman with a strong almost strident voice whose words pour quickly from her mouth bombarding the audience with stories that are best kept hidden from society. The obvious delight Alicia gets from the colourful language and graphic illustrations of her presentations elicits hearty laughter from those watching her perform. It is comedy with a hint of cringe. As she develops her improvisations the shock value of her monologues shifts into some very profound topical social-political commentary. The humour generated remains constant as she angrily deals with feminist issues, racism, nationalism and environmental degradation. She is the performing equivalent of a good caricature cartoonist providing biting commentary in the guise of comedy.

Though there are a lot of similarities between Steve and Alicia's caricature performances, they both have dry humped and disembowelled many real and imagined partners when performing, there are a couple of striking differences. Steve is primarily a physical comic using the Comedia del Arte scenarios of mindless but painless cruelty (no matter how many times the characters are hit over the head they never really seem to be hurt). The deeper meaning in his theatrical presentations comes from the ongoing power struggle between the individual caricatures he portrays.

Alicia uses words to create her caricature and her humour. The comic cruelty is more obviously tinged with disturbing and thought provoking realities. In both cases the vitalising of the spirit that occurs when releasing uncensored, childlike exuberance in physical and vocal play becomes a contagious activity that affects performer and audience alike. This is the most powerful aspect of caricature, its infectious high-spirited humour becomes cathartic when performed well.

I have spoken about three ways a performer can present themselves to an audience. Pedestrian, Character and Caricature are about people, what they look like and how they act. By using the person we are most familiar with, our pedestrian self, as a home base and playing with variations of posture, gesture and voice different characters and caricatures emerge. It is a general rule of thumb that caricature is the most distorted and energised representation of human interaction. Performing pedestrian on the other hand tends to embody a natural and calming energy. Character mode explores a large middle ground between a slight exaggeration of our physical movements and one that is fairly pronounced.

The differing energy inherent in each of these modes offers improvisers a device for varying the emotional dynamic flow of their performance. I once witnessed an Irish storyteller perform for over an hour just sitting in a chair and talking to us, his audience. The main body of his story was spoken in the most natural way (pedestrian mode). Throughout the performance there were judicious shifts into character with corresponding changes of posture, voice and accent that helped to further engage and entertain those watching. The story itself, extremely interesting as it was, became more vibrant because of the storyteller's choice to vary the dynamics by shifting between the performing modes of pedestrian and character.

There is one more mode to deal with, the one I cut my performing teeth on, the one that so attracted me to improvisation, the abstract mode.

ABSTRACT
Abstract is the language of emotion, words the language of content.

In replying to my request for his definition of abstract dancing, a student of mine John Fenelon said, "It is moving without emotion". This was the antithesis of my definition, "expressing emotion through non-literal movement." His preferred method of performing was in caricature. His definition of abstract was not meant to be negative it was just the way he interpreted the term abstract dancing. I must admit I was so taken aback by his statement that I went against one of my own principles of positive feedback (express your thoughts freely without the need to reach agreement) and tried to get John to modify his thoughts and feelings of abstraction to more closely resemble mine.

My wife Lynden's definition is very similar to John's even though her background is modern dance and preferred mode of performance is abstract. We have spent hours discussing our different viewpoints of this term abstract dance. Agreement is not possible and not really necessary. Her feelings while dancing are purely the kinaesthetic feelings of bone and sinew moving precisely through space. She does not experience the shifting moods or hints of character that I do. We do agree, however, that the essence of abstract movement is the non-literal aspect of the movement itself.

In earlier sections of the book I have spoken in depth about how abstract dance so empowered me and in the preceding chapter 'Motion is my Language' detailed how I evolved a methodology of teaching this form of performance presentation. I would now like to present an unusual and probably very controversial interpretation of the use of abstract in performance. It is a personal viewpoint that I am offering as an example of how I use positive feedback to further my development as a teacher and performer.

"Abstract is the language of emotion, words the language of content". I made this statement during a positive feedback session of class when answering a question about why I so enjoy abstract as a performing mode, especially as an audience member. This particular answer proved to be, on a personal level, a very important one for me. It provided an invaluable insight to the way I view performances and helped me in devising several scores that explored ways of combining improvised text and movement.

Because of my hearing loss words (the language of content) have become a blur of indistinguishable sounds. Depending on the acoustics of the room, the volume and enunciation of the performer and my own energy to concentrate I will understand only twenty to fifty percent of the words being spoken. Therefore I get an incomplete picture of any improv that has a proliferation of verbal material. It is not the picture that is incomplete but the content of the story. In fact the picture being presented to me becomes its own story. As my hearing has moved from a moderate loss to a profound one, the story that interests me has become the non-factual or, as I call it the *abstract emotional language*, being presented to me through a performer's posture, distance from the audience, facial movements as well as the speed, volume and pitch of voice when speaking. Because I don't understand the words of a performance I have become attuned to the nuances of movement, voice texture and the story they tell even if the actor is just sitting and talking to the audience.

Words describe the who, what, where, why and when of a situation. The emotions generated by involvement in that situation are communicated through movements of the body and the sound of the voice. Movement, sound, and language when combined together convey a more complete picture of an event than if you isolate one or more of these elements.

I would like to examine a hypothetical situation from several points of view. One in which the cognition of words is absent, another where only words are used to describe the situation and a third where sounds, sight and words combine together to tell the story. Imagine you are travelling in a foreign country and have absolutely no understanding of the language. You chance upon a scene where an extremely agitated woman is describing to a friend how she has just been robbed. You observe their movements and hear their voices but cannot comprehend what is being said. What you see and hear is the different emotional states of the two people involved in this particular situation. The attraction to stop and observe this scenario is the out-of–the-ordinary heightened vocal and visual communication emanating from the woman who has just been robbed. Using your own past experiences you would try to formulate some understanding of why this woman was so distraught. We can see and hear the emotional part of the story but our lack of knowledge of the language being spoken does not allow us to comprehend why the woman is upset.

From her physical gestures, postures, facial expressions and tone of voice you can probably deduce that she is not angry with her friend but with someone else. If you happened to be blind you would be able to hear anger in the sound of her voice even if you couldn't see her. Other emotions such as distress, worry or fear are also communicated through the physicality of the body as well as vocally through the sound of voice. This is the emotional story and it intrigues us to the extent that we would like to know what has happened, what the facts are that caused the emotional outburst from this woman.

Let's take this hypothetical into a more fanciful realm and remove the emotional elements of the story from the factual one. Let's suppose you are given a tape recording of the event in a language that you understand. The words however are spoken in a monotone without variation of pitch, speed or texture. Try reading out loud the next paragraph in a pure monotone, enunciating each syllable to a regular slow pulse beat.

'The man appeared out of nowhere. He knocked me to the ground, grabbed my purse and stood over me with a mad, evil look in his eyes. Then he kicked me viscously in the stomach and walked off laughing towards the school. There was two hundred dollars in my purse. I had just taken the money out of the bank to buy birthday presents for the twins. They're going to be so disappointed. I don't know what to do. I hope the police catch him, lock him up and throw away the key. I would scratch his eyes out if I could. Oh, how am I going to tell Tom about this, he'll be so angry?'

These words have presented you with the facts of the event without your seeing or hearing the emotions of the victim as she relates the story to her friend. Because of the lack of emotional context in presenting the facts I believe you, the listener, will have little if any empathy for the victim's plight. I am deliberately being provocative here by presenting my point of viewing (sic) as a hard of hearing person involved in the performing arts. My way of perceiving spoken language in theatre is not through understanding the content of the story being told but by the emotions being communicated via the body movements and voice sounds of the actor.

On their own can words convey emotion? Read the story again as you would normally read a novel. Was there any difference in your emotional response to the story when read this way than when you read it aloud in a monotone?

The novelist and the poet use only the printed word to tell their stories. We are not presented with movements sounds or visuals to help enhance the emotional impact of what we read. Yet a good writer is able to evoke emotional responses from the reader. But is it just the words you see on paper that creates these emotional responses or is it the skill of the author presenting those words? What is more important for you, the facts presented by words or the emotions conveyed by the way facts are presented? In living our day-to-day lives facts and emotions go hand in glove with each other. They intermingle in a natural and in most cases unpremeditated way. Within the performing arts however a more deliberate integration of information and emotional dynamics is orchestrated by the creators of the performance piece.

Let's go back to that hypothetical example, put it into the hands of a playwright, actor and director, and ask them to turn this scenario into a play so that it can be relived on stage. They will combine their skills to bring together the emotional and factual elements of the story. This is in essence what most scripted plays are all about, actors portraying people, acting out situations with varying degrees of emotional intensity. A good author shapes the words and relationships between characters in such a way that the emotional integrity of the play is enhanced; good actors, through skilful use of movement and voice, make the characters they are portraying emotionally real; and a good director works with actors and writer to combine the emotional story (physical movements and vocal use of the actor) with the factual story (the writer's script) into a theatrically exciting presentation. In any play, as in real life, the two stories, emotional and factual, are happening simultaneously, though not always in equal proportion. A director will orchestrate how these stories intermingle, sometimes letting the facts predominate at other times letting the movement, music, sound or lighting set an emotional tone.

Until I called abstract 'the language of emotion' all of my teaching dealt with abstract occurring through movement or by speaking in fractured disjointed sentences. This new look allowed me to adapt my use of abstract to exploring ways of developing an ability to work in character mode. I found that by assuming various postures and speaking with a subtle but unusual texture to my voice I could create interesting monologues as a character, something that had eluded me until then.

And so character has been added to the modalities I have available to use in my performances. It is a lovely addition allowing me to include words, the language of content to emotional moods that I feel while doing an abstract movement piece. This has taken me another step further away from the beautiful abstract dance theatre pieces choreographed by my mentor Alwin Nikolais who once wrote, "To me, the art of drama is one thing; the art of theatre is another. In the latter, a magical panorama of things, sounds, colours, shapes, lights, illusions and events happen before your eyes and ears. I find my needs cannot be wholly satisfied by one art." [6]

Since my work with Terry Sendgraff and Ruth Zaporah and their explorations in the use of language in improvisations I too am not satisfied working in just one art form or just one performing mode. My need has been to combine all the performing arts (music, dance and theatre) using all four modes (pedestrian, character, caricature and abstract) as my means of communication.

Of course it was not always this way. I started with abstract dance and for more than a decade that was my sole means of communication. I can recall my first improvisation using abstract movement and remember the flying feeling of release as my body immediately gave voice to this soundless language, a language that allowed me to communicate unconscious emotions and started me on a journey that will take me to the end of my life.

[6] *The Modern Dance – Seven Statements of Belief,* Ed. Selma Jeanne Cohen
Wesleyan University Press, Middletown, Connecticut 1965

Stillness. Arms up, elbows bent, jagged lines vibrating in an erratic rhythm. Fall sideways. Roll up sitting on heels, back fully arched, head straining even further backwards, the skin stretched tightly over Adam's apple. Head jerking side to side, arms rising, falling, reaching, bending, straightening. Shapes predominantly jagged and angular, rhythms irregular. Walls and corners offer a haven where my body curls up with limbs distorted in fitful resting. Locomotion is awkward, ungainly, limping noticeable. The body screams silently with a visible volume that is deafening. I am dancing. I am alive. I am happy.

7

The *EN* Game
(Our *EN*-tertaining Ways)

*En*tertain, *en*gage, *en*lighten, *en*rich, *en*dear, *en*gross, *en*trance, *en*noble, *en*ergize, *en*chant, *en*rapture, *en*thral, *en*thuse, *en*tice are all words that reflect how a performer might like to effect an audience. Performers certainly *en*trap an audience by luring them into their d*en* with various advertisements that *en*sure what is witnessed will be *en*joyable. I like to think of the word *en*tertain as the mother word from which all the other *en* words spring, defining the various ways we have of pleasing an audience. I know some performing artists do not like to classify themselves as entertainers and I do respect that. There is, however, the old adage of low-brow and high-brow entertainment, a terminology which signifies one can be entertained in several different ways. Whether a performance deals with music, dance or drama, whether what we see is broad slapstick or a serious representation of war and its repercussions, we as audience members go to the theatre to be entertained in some way. What entertains us is a matter of individual aesthetics.

In the second half of my extended performance workshops we look at four possible ways of entertaining an audience: *humour, expertise, challenge (physical or emotional) and beauty*. By isolating, combining and shifting between these elements the improvising performer can more easily create structure to help elongate a performance. This is especially the case when used in conjunction with the four modes of performing. Let's take a look at each entertaining way separately and then see how they might combine with one another to form a greater whole.

HUMOUR: Making an audience laugh is a very gratifying experience and is the means of entertaining most students initially use. Laughter lets the performer know that the audience is appreciating the presentation. The confidence which students gain from hearing laughter allows them to stay in the present instead of being concerned about boring the audience. As a student grows in confidence the need for the instant gratification one gets from hearing an audience laugh is diminished. There is a natural movement towards other ways of maintaining interest and a willingness to deal with material that is of a more serious nature.

There are several ways of persuading an audience to laugh through the use of one's physicality:

-- Rhythmic walking with undulations of the spine and/or various manners of bobbing and weaving with the head. You can add some well-timed asides to the audience with a knowing look on your face.

-- Silly walks, as hilariously demonstrated by John Cleese in Monty Python's Flying Circus, are simply a series of non-sequential awkward steps done in character or caricature mode.

-- An elongated run around the studio, exhibiting signs of heavy breathing, tiredness, exhaustion. Almost coming to a stop but picking up the run again and again is always good for a laugh.

-- Choosing a particular spot in the room where you always trip over an imaginary object. This can be a constant happening throughout a long piece. Once the pattern is established there can be some very long gaps between the trip-ups.

-- Well-timed erratic speeding up, slowing down and stopping.

-- Shifting between a floppy and more normal use of the body using a skilful use of timing is also good for a laugh.

-- Using opposites in a judicious way, changing between heroic and pathetic postures, can earn a few chuckles if done with the correct comic timing.

Comic timing is the key to most humour. Some people seem to have the gift of comedy. Others have to explore and experiment with timing, often experiencing several failures before they find what works for them. Timing depends more on the eccentricities of the character being presented than on a set number of counts before delivering the punch line. It is definitely a felt not a counted thing.

Caricature mode itself is a rich vein of comedy. The ridiculous over-the-top physicality and vocality (sic) inherent in this mode almost always ensures a good laugh.

The spoken word is the way most of us express humour. We often talk about someone being satirical, droll, ironic or witty when referring to language that we find amusing. Students in my classes develop their own style of verbal comedy through growing into it. The natural humour that arises when performers put themselves in the vulnerable position of facing an audience without planning anything always seems to work better than the premeditated joke.

EXPERTISE: Skills in dance, gymnastics, music, singing, comedy, dialogue, character creation, clowning and choreography are all appreciated by an audience. The greater the level of expertise the greater the entertainment value.

Other than fostering a more articulate use of physicality I do not 'teach' expertise in my workshops. I deal with it during the one-on-one sessions I have with students, helping each one to recognise his or her own form of expertise, encouraging them to use and develop these as a means to entertain an audience. While some students already have well-developed skills others have very little experience in the performing arts. I find it interesting that some highly trained dancers and singers avoid using their developed skills in improvisation because they say they are bored with what they can already do, and that they have come to my classes to 'add something new' to their repertoires. I tell them to pay attention to their own words, that adding something new to one's skill base does not mean exchanging one skill for another.

In the extended workshops the fact that students must present thirty minutes of material allows for both well-developed skills and emerging ones to be performed. Even for those students who do not have an advanced expertise to exhibit it is still important to work with the performing skills they have already learned. Entertaining and engagement elements of performances come from different areas. As they continue working with improvisational performance students will choose particular skills that suit their personalities and seek out teachers to help develop an expertise in the areas they most enjoy.

CHALLENGE: Remember going to the circus and being thrilled by the high-wire act? Certainly I appreciated the balancing skills of the wirewalker, however the major attraction for me was not the virtuosity exhibited but the death-defying height at which the tricks were performed. Except for clowns, circus performers primarily depend on acts where the main form of entertainment is physical challenge. The strong man, the contortionist, the juggler are constantly working to lift more weight, bend their limbs beyond the imaginable, or juggle that one extra ball.

Performers can also engage us by taking the emotional risk of presenting very personal material: we can be enriched by a performance that emotionally challenges us with something we might find unpleasant. Terry Sendgraff succeeded in this the first time she performed after a radical mastectomy of her left breast. Starting off in total darkness, swinging on her trapeze while the lights slowly came up, she was dressed only in a loincloth, her single full breast exposed for all to see. At first all seemed perfectly normal, as Terry was swinging side-on to the audience. Only those of us who knew Terry anticipated with some trepidation what would happen next. As she slowly rotated on the trapeze the audience as one let out an audible gasp as they realised they were about to participate in a one-hour show with a one-breasted woman. Nudity can entertain through beauty and or sexual titillation. In this case the emotional challenge Terry took to expose herself and her audience to a scarred and deformed woman, something most people want to keep hidden was a very enlightening and enriching experience.

Doing something physically challenging is clearly a human trait. We all love a challenge otherwise we would never have learnt to walk or talk. Most of us enjoy being witness to physical challenges and attend sporting events, enjoy reading about people who overcome physical injuries, applaud with wide-eyed amazement the death-defying acts of circus performers. Likewise, opera and ballet are enjoyed not only for their artistic merits but also for the dancers' physical skills and the power and pitch range of the singers' voices.

A score of gentle and not so gentle pulling and pushing is a means of experiencing the entertainment value of physical challenge. An important element is to make sure that students do not create the situation of a competitive wrestling match but stay true to the physical activity of pulling and pushing, using any and all parts of the body with as much force as they can muster safely. What evolves is a playful exhibition of peoples' bodies straining against each other in all sorts of shapes and configurations some funny, some beautiful with attending grunts, groans, smiles and laughter.

One of my favourite scores is working in extreme medium speed. This exercise offers a unique challenge. I enjoy presenting this oxymoron to students as a means of getting them to explore the midpoint between extremely slow and extremely fast. They are not allowed to speed up or slow down, all movements even the steps they take in walking must stay in an even-paced medium speed. This takes a lot of concentration and physical control. It is more challenging than the pulling and pushing score. The resulting grace creates a meditative, thoughtful and mesmerising movement motif somewhat similar to that of t'ai chi.

Many a time I have heard people say, 'that was a risky thing to do', referring to an improvising performer expressing an emotionally charged subject. Yet the performers would often reply that they did not feel at risk and were actually in an inspired state at the time. In writing a review for *The Age* newspaper about an evening of improvised performance Vicki Fairfax stated, "There is much talk among improvisers about risk taking. But, paradoxically, there seems to be less risk here than in conventional performances that must work with the constraints of choreography, script, lighting cues and an audience with a container load of preconceptions about what they are here to see. The risk here is about being unable to relinquish control". I found this a very astute comment. Just the act of performing is an extremely vulnerable thing to do. There is a risk factor in both improvisation and well-rehearsed performance. The concern within a set piece of theatre is that of fluffing a rehearsed step or line whereas the concern of the improviser is actually being too concerned about getting things 'right'.

While doing one of my extended performing workshops, Sally Smith, an accomplished dancer and talented singer, expressed her anxiety about feeling stuck. She lacked confidence in being impulsive and this is such a necessary element of improvisation. We talked about emotional risk-taking and when an improviser feels most at risk. The improviser feels most vulnerable when she is in what I call a search state of mind. There are two other states of mind that the improviser can experience while performing: the working state and the inspired state. When in search mode, the performer is in the process of looking for material they can develop. This is the most uncomfortable phase for an improviser and usually happens at the beginning of a performance but can reappear later, especially in longer pieces. When in a working state of mind the performer is consciously using his or her skills, working hard to develop a theatrical event. When in the inspired state of mind, that elusive Holy Grail, you feel as if you are being moved by the performance rather than moving it yourself. It seems as if nothing can go wrong and that you are on the outside observing something wonderful taking place even though you are the one on the inside creating it.

We also spoke about the art versus therapy conundrum. She was anxious about what would emerge in a performance if she were not in control. I told her that in my many years of experience no one had ever revealed anything they did not want to and more often than not the revelations were done in character, caricature or abstract modes thereby creating a theatrical event not a therapy session. I also proposed that she begin her next few classroom performances doing nothing and thinking of nothing. This is probably the biggest emotional risk a performer can take, doing nothing. Why? Because people have paid to see us do something and we feel a responsibility to give them their money's worth.

Actually it is impossible to do nothing. Some part of us is always moving even when we think we are standing still. It might be a softening or hardening of the cheek, a slight raising of the eyebrow. Our weight can shift just that tiny bit from our left to our right foot. Perhaps the head will turn a degree or two or the back relaxes or the fingers bend a little. I asked Sally to pay attention to these usually unfelt movements and with the least amount of conscious thought possible choose which ones to expand, adding soft melodic tones or short snatches of song if she wished. Basically I wanted her to listen to her movements, talk to herself through movement, and let the mood of the moment express itself to her before she expressed it to the audience.

This seemed to work for Sally. During her thirty minute showcase solo performance in front of an audience that included family, friends and strangers she ended her piece with ten minutes of an exquisitely improvised blues style melody, vocally accompanying her deliciously soulful dancing. She let herself go, gave up trying to do a good performance and ended up in the inspired state of a great one. And she was beautiful!

BEING BEAUTIFUL OR PROFOUND: By far the most difficult way for an improviser to express oneself in front of an audience is by being beautiful. In this mode, we make ourselves extremely vulnerable. Fearing rejection, we avoid exhibiting ourselves in a beautiful way, more often than not choosing humour and expertise as ways of presentation. And yet beauty is one of the most pleasant ways of being entertained. All my initial attempts at

trying to get people to be beautiful in their performances ended in failure until one of my students, Bronwen Barton, who was also my singing teacher, insisted that I include the word "profound" in my search for performance beauty. This was the key. Someone expressing something that is of real importance to them can often create a theatrical moment

about which audience members will say, 'I found that very moving, very beautiful'.

These ways of entertaining an audience are developed in the second half of the extended performance workshop. I often use the four modes of performance as tools for working on the different ways of entertaining. This allows students to continue practicing their work in the modes as well as adding some new insights into varying their performances dynamically.

At first we deal with shifting between opposites, finding transitions between movement and language, between being serious and being silly. Shifting between pedestrian, character and caricature modes while presenting a five-minute monologue quite often allows the student to naturally move between the humorous and profound content. Speaking in pedestrian mode generally produces an atmosphere of thoughtful reminiscence. The shift to character or caricature tends to add moments of light-hearted or even outrageous comedy.

Similarly, a dance piece that shifts between the modes of abstract, character and caricature has the potential to be beautiful as well as humorous and to include high levels of expertise and physical challenge. Let me elaborate further.

And she was beautiful! Watching Sally Smith's solo performance I was entertained by my perception of something profound being beautifully expressed by a highly skilled performer who was taking a risk and expressing her emotions of the moment in the most exquisitely theatrical way. The only way I was not being entertained was through the use of humour. Yes it was my perception of beauty and as the old saying goes, 'beauty is in the eyes of the beholder'. So what is beauty? How does one achieve it? There are no definitive answers to these questions. We each have our own sense and feeling of what is beautiful and even that might change from day to day. To achieve something that is so elusive is quite a daunting task. Trying to be beautiful, profound or funny when improvising often backfires. True humour or beauty can be found only when an improviser stops trying and simply expresses herself wholeheartedly whatever her emotional state of being is at the moment.

So how can I as a performer entertain you? You are my audience and have paid money to be *en*gaged, *en*lightened, *en*tranced, *en*ergised, *en*tertained by me. You might be a friend, a colleague or a total stranger. In fact you, the audience, are an entity that contains a mixture of people all with different tastes and opinions on what constitutes 'good theatre'. You, the audience, are a singularity with multiple personalities so which one of you am I supposed to entertain?

The answer is a complex one yet it can be stated very simply. The answer is me! I am the one I most want to please. This is not as egocentric as it sounds. Knowing I cannot please all of the people all of the time I must choose between developing my performance style to please people whose theatrical tastes are different from mine or those whose are similar. Making this choice allows me to at least please some of the people some of the time. As an improviser who takes on the multiple roles of creator, director and performer the decision of what I practice and how I develop is mine alone. Yes there will be consultations with people whose aesthetics I admire, development of skills through studying with teachers whose work I find valuable and reflections on the effect my performances have on various audiences. So, if it were possible for me as the creator/director to be part of the audience that was watching me the performer, in essence it is that person (the creator/director) I would most want to please.

This seemingly self-centred orientation is an important step in order to ascertain, acknowledge and develop one's aesthetic principles. However, unless I want to perform for an audience of one (myself) I must continue to augment the necessary skills of theatrical communication that will allow me in the long term to please most of the people most of the time.

It is the recognition of possibilities in the way performers present themselves through the four modes of performance and the several ways of entertainment that allows improvisers to modulate the dynamic structure of their performance. We can put these eight elements: pedestrian, character, caricature, abstract, humour, expertise, challenge and beauty into a hat. Then by intuitively choosing, shifting and combining their use a marriage between impulse and form is completed. Though improvisers do not know what they are going to do they do know what they are doing and can recognize and develop emerging structures. It is this endless search for and practice of the various elements that create theatre that is the cornerstone of the improvising performer. We do not work on developing a particular theatre piece but hone our skills to be able to create a spontaneous performance from an infinite number of possibilities. Hence Ruth Zaporah's classic statement "I have planned nothing and spent a long time doing it."[7]

---

[7] Ibid A statement on a flier Ruth Zaporah used for one of her performance series.

8
EYE to EYE

Our deepest fear is not that we are inadequate.
Our deepest fear is that we are powerful beyond measure.[8]

I refuse to teach my students how to become better performers. I leave that responsibility up to them. This is based on my aesthetic and philosophical belief that enhancing one's self as an improviser requires the student to find and evolve a style of presentation and content that is uniquely theirs. Warren Burt, one of my long-time students, wrote an article about my teaching style that he called 'Teaching Without Teaching'.[9] Certainly students come to my classes to learn the craft of improvisation but the methodology of positive feedback I employ obliges them to become both teacher and student. This method forms the foundation of my work. What I want to impart is the joy of improvisation and the value of positive feedback as a phenomenally insightful self-teaching and learning tool.

My insistence that students only talk about the positive aspects they experience while doing an exercise, or what elements they enjoy while watching a performance, is my way of reawakening them to the fact that they are their own best teachers. The choice of this approach lies in the concept of using performance as a means of developing the performer. The more accepted form of critique advises performers on how to enhance the performance. When I was a student of dance composition my teachers' comments focused on what I should do in order to create a more substantial choreographic work. Feedback was concerned with improving the bottom line, the performance itself, smoothing out the wrinkles so that on opening night everything would be as perfect as possible.

---

[8] Nelson Mandela (1994 Inaugural speech)
[9] MUSICWORKS explorations in sound # 76 spring 2000

Even as an improvising performer most of the post-performance feedback I have received from audience members has been along the lines of what they thought would have been better left out or their wish that I had stayed with a particular section longer because in their opinion it was so beautiful. In other words what they might have done in order to improve the performance. But the performance, being an improvised one, would never be repeated and therefore could not be improved upon. Improvisers can never improve a performance the only thing they can work on is improving the performer. In improvisation it is the performer who is the end product, the bottom line that an audience comes to see.

Philosophy Of Positive Feedback

Initially I conceived positive feedback as a means of alleviating the negative judgement that can crop up in the middle of a performance. If an improvising performer gets into the mind space of, 'Shit, this isn't working, what do I do now?' they are indeed in deep shit. They are no longer in the present but have fallen into the trap of judging negatively something that has already happened. The imposition of judgement over one's self can slow down and even stop the intuitive creative process. Introducing a style of critique where people talk about a single event or ongoing happening they found enjoyable helps to alleviate a negative state of mind. At any one moment there will be things that we can both like and dislike in our performance. Focusing our feedback on what is going right rather than what is going wrong forces the negative judge that sits on one shoulder to take a back seat to the positive voice on the other.

Of even more importance is the fact that positive feedback helps reawaken the creative teacher residing in all of us. The best teacher you ever had or ever will have is yourself. Cast your mind back to when you were between the ages of nought to two and learnt to walk and talk. Think about the process you went through in order to achieve these skills. You did not go to school, hire private tutors or read books. You were your own teacher -

experimenting, exploring and getting wonderful positive feedback from your caregivers. From almost everyone, young or old, who happened to cross your path, a playful interchange of movement and sounds ensued, a duet with an underlying agenda to help (not teach) you develop your own style of walking and talking. Inevitably there were smiles, laughter and lots of cuddles as you taught yourself these skills.

I continually use my experience of being present during a child's first steps as an example of positive feedback. I have been involved in this ritual twice. On both occasions several adults were present when the child decided to perform the newly learned skill. Although these events were separated by seventeen years, the scenario for each was exactly the same. When the adults realised what was happening, they all sat in a circle. The young performer teetered and wobbled from the outstretched arms of one adult to another - Ooo's, ahs, smiles, cheers and hand claps all around the circle. There was a huge, beaming smile on the child's face. Not a single adult thought of saying, 'That was lovely (insert your own name), now if you could just hold your back a little straighter and lift your knees higher, you will walk even better the next time'. Why not? The child certainly was not walking well. Yet we, the adults, knew that the child would continue to develop the skills of walking, running, skipping, hopping and other forms of exciting locomotion. It is important that student improvisers return to this atmosphere of playful exploration they had as young children, the time in life when our impulsive behaviour is at its peak.

There are two major compartments in the improviser's tool bag, impulse and form. Of these two, impulse is the more valuable. It is the spanner that unbolts the unconscious, that pries open the doorways to fresh ideas and helps to find new patterns of physical and vocal behaviour. It is this freedom to play which infuses both performer and audience with the exciting energy of searching for and discovering magic moments of theatre that give improvised performance its unique flavour:

*I want to run as fast as I can! I want to jump high!
I want to make lots of sounds. I want to stop. I
want to yell. I need to catch my breath. I want to
shake my hands, to lift them high over my head and
spin around until I laugh. I like speaking in voices
that are gruff, melodious, soft and loud, creating a
musical prose that is abstract and literal at the
same time. I cannot do the things I want to do if I
allow myself to be governed by the need to
conform to someone else's criteria of what
constitutes a good performance. I must give myself
the freedom to take the risk of so-called failure.
For without taking that risk I will get bogged
down, repeating formulae that I perceive to work
well. And then that which makes improvisation so
exciting to me, that moment of performed
revelation, will be lost from my vocabulary.*

Most students do not trust their impulsive child and fall into the trap of needing to do something 'good' in order to please others. Too often students try to emulate someone else's style because it seems to be popular. By taking this copycat route the best they can hope for is an inferior version of that other person's style: an attempted mirror image that is only surface deep. Many of us tend to play it safe, sticking to some learned or perceived blueprint of what is a good performance. By trying to do something 'good', (usually the teacher's good) we deny ourselves the freedom to search for our own aesthetic values and are left with a poor imitation of another person's creative genius.

Developing confidence in the genius that lives inside our own mind is the only way that we can value and evolve the style of presentation that most suits us. This is an essential reason for positive feedback being an integral part of workshop practice, beginning with the very first workshop every student attends. It is why I have students spend their first year being as impulsively playful as they can. This is extremely difficult. It is especially so for those with extensive training in any of the performing arts.

These particular students have trained hard and developed valuable skills that are greatly admired by an audience and they do not want to give all that up. But it is not the skills they have to give up. In fact it is impossible for well-trained people to eliminate the techniques they find meaningful. It is the need to impress, to show off, to make sure one is doing something worthwhile that gets in the way of developing confidence in the spontaneous generation of ideas, movements, sounds and words. For the improvising performer it is essential that the unconscious, intuitive part of the personality must be given the work time needed to reveal itself and develop the confidence that extraordinarily good things can emerge while being freely impulsive.

Being impulsive is just the beginning of the process of developing the improviser. One must also be able to elaborate the impulse well enough so that clear structures emerge. The marriage of form to impulse has to occur in order to create theatre that is accessible and enjoyable. To develop structure and form, students must acknowledge, value and evolve their own personal power sources. Positive feedback is again the important influence here. The conscious work of developing one's self as an improvising performer commences with the search for these personal power sources. Simply put, in many words, a power source is what you like, enjoy, gives you pleasure, turns you on, excites you, a thing that you do easily, something you do unconsciously and frequently, a pattern of physical behaviour, your personal philosophies, personality traits, anything that empowers you. Everyone has several personal power sources and there are countless possibilities of what a power source might be.

To facilitate the search for and development of power sources I have incorporated four areas of positive feedback in the class structure. These comprise the partnering section of class, the witnessed doing and watching, the performer's feedback and the audience feedback. In the partnering section of class students explore and experience movement within the parameters of given scores. There is no audience. This allows for a freer unselfconscious state of play. Doing these exercises enables students to ascertain several things about themselves: whether they prefer moving at fast, slow or medium speeds; what sort of shapes they enjoy making; if their preference is for working internally or extending their energies outwards; if they prefer to initiate ideas or respond to the actions of others. After each exercise the partners stay in their pairings and give each other feedback about what movement or relationship aspect of the duet they enjoyed or found of value. Over a period of time, after doing many scores with many partners, students  begin to recognise patterns emerging in themselves. If a particular element of enjoyment keeps appearing time and time again a student's continuing feedback on the same topic will guide him or her to the fact that a personal power source is at play.

Several unique sources have presented themselves during classes over the years. One student had an amazing head of long, thick, curly blond hair. Here was the physical reincarnation of the fairytale character Rapunzel. The student used the shape and weight of her hair all the time in her performances. Then there was Sean the gymnast. After a period of two years I finally realised that what I found unique about his dancing was that most of his movements had a sideways orientation. This gave even his most abstract movements a sense of mischievousness. Or take Michael Green whose power sources include working low to the ground. In his early improvisations Michael's beginnings consisted of walking in circles in a search for what to do. He would seem totally lost then for no apparent reason would suddenly lower himself to the ground and, as if he had turned a switch on, would become completely involved in what he was doing and present a beautifully constructed abstract movement piece that was very animalistic in nature.

I list my own personal power sources as hands, locomotion, space shaping, Hum Drumming, vocal sounds, autobiographical stories, isolated movements and timing. It is the mixing and matching of these elements that creates my performing persona. I do not however, limit myself to these theatrical ploys though I continue to develop them. I am still looking for hidden power sources, and enjoy those that are evolving as my physicality changes. The ongoing search for new and different elements allows me to grow as an ageing performer. Whereas once I used to love jumping, tumbling, speed and strength-oriented movements, time, a knee replacement and an arthritic back have taken those joys away from me to be replaced by some of the less physically challenging power sources mentioned above.

Slowing down the need to improve as improvisers actually speeds up the development of this particular form of theatre. The confidence in being impulsive in the performing space can be short-circuited when one rushes to develop the first personal power source to emerge. If students begin developing that initial power source they will put limits on impulsive play, inhibiting the possibility of finding others. I advise students to hold off increasing the skill levels of the first power source they recognise and continue with playful explorations of movement, sounds and words as a means of seeking out more sources. This helps develop a trust that valuable material will constantly emerge from their impulsive behaviour, thereby solidifying confidence in their own spontaneity. After three or four power sources have been acknowledged it is then time to focus on each one, enhancing the skills associated with them and finding out how they mix and match with each other. This shifting between and blending of power sources becomes the students' personal style of self-presentation in the performing space and, along with an underlying faith in the intuitive process, the melding of impulse and form is then complete.

Style, the sum of the many different elements that go into the way performers present themselves, is where the relationship between impulse and form begins to manifest itself. Recognising and understanding movement and language patterns that continually emerge from our impulses commences the process of developing an improviser's uniqueness in the performing arena. In particular it is the skill development of the power sources that raises a student's base level of 'goodness', or 'authentic proficiency' if you like. This base level increases with the acquisition of technical skills in the areas of movement, voice, and stagecraft. The evolution of these skills allows the student to become a jack of all performing trades, which to some extent all improvisers must become, and enhances their ability to engage an audience. This is why the positive feedback question 'Why do you like doing what you do?' is so important, for it is within the answer to the question 'why?' that learning emerges.

Take for example someone whose power source is locomotion, the enjoyment of travelling through space. An answer to the question, 'Why locomotion?' might be the sense of power felt in the legs, especially when covering long distances quickly (space gobbling) and the dramatic changes that occur when approaching or leaving someone. From this answer a few simple scores can be devised that can help embellish this activity. For example: exploring various uses of the legs and feet and varying the size and speed of the steps to increase the variety of locomotion possibilities; playing with when, where and how to come to a stop; working with different types of pathways, straight line, circular, zigzag, or erratic; possibly changing between pedestrian, character and abstract modes. This all helps increase the physical vocabulary of the space gobbler, which in turn enhances theatrical and emotional range.

The 'doing and watching' section of class is designed to demonstrate the theatrical value of sticking to a task. This is usually done after having the class work on small group scores, which have a theatrical or inter-relationship theme. Initially the groups simultaneously play within the parameters given without anyone watching. I then have each group do another exploration of the score while the other groups observe. Those who are doing are not to perform for those watching but to relate to each other as if they were not being witnessed. This allows for the watchers to judge for themselves the value of certain theatrical skills. The Facings and Spacings score is particularly useful in this respect. I created it to give students practice in developing visual and dramatic interest through varying the distances and the body facings (back to back, front to front, back to side, etc.) between partners. Watching others exercise this skill allows students to see its importance as an element of stagecraft. It is only through watching others explore spacings and facings that one can truly sense the theatrical validity of the device.

Since I want to reinforce the fact that the exercise is a doing and not a performance I have the watchers only give feedback. Improvisers must enhance their external eye, the inner-director, who informs the choices made spontaneously and helps add subtlety and colour to performance content. Without this eye, impulsive play would lack structure and coherence. Finding the words that describe the value inherent in a specific theatrical component is the basic skill of a director, who must be able to convey to the performer the importance of the theatrical ploys being used to enhance a performance.

The remaining two forms of feedback, the performer's and the audience's, take place during the performance section of class. There are no scores or themes given prior to performance and students are strongly encouraged to enter the performing space devoid of ideas about what they wish to do. I call this total improvisation, the spontaneous creation of a cohesive theatre piece. After performing, each performer sits on the 'feedback cushion' facing the rest of the group, the audience, and gives feedback about what he or she enjoyed doing during their solo or duet. The object is to identify, express, and gain valuable insight into what emerges impulsively when in the performance state of mind. Choosing a particular moment or an ongoing quality within the performance to talk about, helps pinpoint those elements of theatre which are most meaningful to the performer. It also begins the process of focusing the performer's mind on what is enjoyable at the moment of theatrical conception. To isolate and understand what one likes during a performance will eventually lead to elongating and adding substance to an initial impulse. Whilst performing, a structure emerges from the recognition of what is enjoyable in the moment and one can use this as a base to develop the theme and variations of emerging material.

After the performer feedback is completed, audience members then have the opportunity to voice theirs. Here also, talking about the performance as a whole, how good, funny or beautiful it was is really of little value either to the performer or the audience member giving the feedback. I want students who have watched to use what I call 'outside feedback' to develop their inner director. The comments they give to someone else's performance should be for themselves. Trying to ascertain what the performer actually did with movement, voice, or face that made you laugh or cry in empathy is the type of feedback that compels the watcher to 'see' the myriad of detail which creates comedy or pathos. It is the ability to isolate the various elements and understand how to knit them together to form an interesting and entertaining theatre piece that is the art of the director. *It*, the performance as a whole, is like a gourmet meal: the blending of flavours, the art of choosing ingredients, the skill of cooking, and the craft of presenting the food, all combine to make eating it a marvellous experience.

Impulse and style beget content. Content is the last of a three-link chain in the development of the improvising performer. The first and strongest link is the confidence to be impulsive. The second link, style, grows out of the first and provides form and substance to inspiration. Content is the message we wish to communicate to the world. It is the realm of the playwright, composer and choreographer. I ask students not to be concerned about content until they have spent some time developing their style. I believe it is through the use of impulsive play that we find out what we truly want to say. If we approach a performance with a preconceived notion of what the content should be we will have closed the doors to the unconscious and semiconscious material within ourselves. Impulsive play is the key that unlocks the doors to our less conscious selves and allows us to do more of what we want to do and less of what we think we should do. I am not saying that consciousness is a bad thing in improvisation. It is a very valuable tool as long as it is used in conjunction with the more spontaneous part of our being.

131

The improviser who performs without preconception never knows what message or method will prevail in any particular performance. If the sequence of development has been from impulse to style to content, the artist will be communicating personal stories in some way, shape or form. Creative artists have only their experiences to call upon and use as material for script, dance piece or music composition. The subtext of any personal story is its social and political relevance. How we view ourselves in relationship to society, our environment and past historical moments of our lives becomes the content of our communication. How we perform this content, directly, indirectly, abstractly, through use of voice or language or movement is totally up to the individual and his or her style of presentation.

Many people think that being personal on stage smacks too much of therapy and that 'therapy is not art'. I agree that therapy is not the same thing as art, however, it is my belief that art, therapy and communication are interwoven. Art is definitely therapeutic to the arts practitioner. It is a means many people use to express themselves through the medium of their choice in any of the visual or performing arts. People undergoing therapy are asked to communicate their feelings freely. The basic difference is the unwritten contract that exists between therapist and client and between teacher and art student. The therapist seeks to heal clients by helping them to get in touch with and express feelings. Students of art seek out a teacher who will help them develop the language of painting, sculpture, dance, music or drama. In essence both client and student are seeking help in communication techniques. Seen in this light, positive feedback is a communication tool; between social self and theatrical self, between student and teacher, between artist and mentor.

There is good therapy and bad therapy. There is good art and bad art. Good therapy occurs when the participant is able to clearly communicate feelings. Good art occurs when the artist exhibits a well-developed command of a medium's techniques. Great art occurs through the ability to combine clear and uninhibited emotional statements with the highly evolved skill levels of the professional practitioner.

Most people immediately assume 'emotional statements' implies the heightened emotional states of hate, love, anger, fear and joy. I believe it is this assumption that causes people to say 'you should not bring your therapy into your performance'. It is as if they are afraid of an overlong blast of an extreme emotion that never reaches resolution. The reality is that most of the time our emotional experiences are not extreme. Contented, thoughtful, perplexed, bemused, light-hearted, describe some of the states of our medium emotional range. A good artist uses colour well, musicians have an amazing digital dexterity, and dancers an agility, athleticism and total body awareness. If you add an ability to express a wide range of emotional experiences to the physical skill/technique of the artist, then we enter the realm of good or even great art. If you also add the ability to perform spontaneously we are now talking about the art of the improviser.

Practical Steps To Developing Positive Feedback

Name *it*. Describe *it*. What did you like about *it*? If you can do these three things you will be on the road to giving valuable positive feedback. But what is *it*? Quite often a student will say of a performance 'I loved *it*', or 'I found *it* beautiful', or '*it* made me laugh'. The response, though quite valid, is very general, it lacks detail. Students of the performing arts must go beyond the surface of how a performance affected them. It is in perceiving and articulating a particular moment or ongoing happening within an improvisation, a specific detail that we can isolate and work on, that will help us develop our own ability as improvisers. The positive feedback method is a lifelong journey that seeks to name the infinite number of elements that are inherent in a single moment of theatre. I ask of my students that they take on the challenge of developing a descriptive language. This becomes the device that their inner director uses to help structure improvisation. It also trains the teacher within to isolate and create exercises that develop technical skills and help the performing self embrace the style that suits him or her best. Essentially then, the total improvisation we do in my classes demands of the students that they wear all three hats, the director's, the teacher's and the performer's.

After twenty years of developing positive feedback as a learning tool I began to feel there was something lacking in the way I presented the concept. In reality all I had been doing for those two decades was evolving some very good reasons for validating the use of positive feedback and constantly asking two questions: 'What did you like?' and 'Why did you like it?' Finally I realised that I needed to include more specific, equally important questions, such as 'What did you see?' 'What was the performer doing that engaged you?' 'Can you put a name to it?' As a consequence of this I decided to run an intensive program on positive feedback itself for the mutual benefit of both me and my students.

The title I gave to the first workshop, held in the spring of 2001, was *Eye to Eye: Insights to Improvisation*. It began with a man walking. I asked the participants to write down five observations about the walking man, using three words or less for each observation. I performed the walking in the most neutral and non-theatrical way possible. The following is a small list of some of the answers given.

Direction.....Even pulse.....Direction of attention

Balance and Weight Shift.....Gentle swinging arms

Weight in body.....A man looking

The essence of this exercise was to illustrate that everyone sees things differently and to have students realise that even a very simple physical activity such as walking contains several different elements that can be observed and named. Being able to see, name and describe the things people see as they watch performances; to sense, name, and describe what we ourselves do while performing can help override the tendency to judge a performance as 'good' or 'bad'.

Naming things helps in creating a vocabulary that brings to consciousness the huge variety of elements that are inherent in any theatre piece, be it music, dance or drama. I'll paraphrase an old philosophical conundrum, the question of whether a tree can exist without someone around who can see it. I offer another conundrum to speculate upon. Can a tree exist if it doesn't have a name? A performance is like a forest filled with various trees, shrubs, birds, animals and insects that interact together to form an environment that most people find exquisitely beautiful. If we were asked to create our own woodlands we would have to know the different trees, insects, birds and animals, in other words their names, and have an understanding of how they interact with each other to form a holistic environment. Similarly, improvising performers must have an awareness of how to combine the separate elements of theatre and performance into a holistic package but, before they can do that, they must know what these elements are. This is the importance of having a language that names and describes the things we can see. The more names and descriptions we can accurately create the deeper the understanding of what we are seeing.

My advice to students is that they use as few words as possible to name and define the various aspects of theatre they have enjoyed. Simplifying tends to make descriptions more colourful and richer in context. Students who search for and find their own words will create a vocabulary that will be much more meaningful to them than unthinkingly using someone else's language. I also advise them to plagiarise freely any name or descriptive phase that they find valuable. This is what makes language interesting and unites us as individuals in a society, this sharing in the development of words that help us to understand each other and the world around us.

What we perceive is usually a reflection of our personal aesthetics. I want students to recognise that stating the simple and obvious is an important first step in achieving a feedback system that will give them insight into developing themselves as performers. By looking at some of the answers to 'the man walking' exercise, and taking it to a deeper level by asking 'What interested you about a particular observation?' the improviser begins the journey to understanding his or her own performing style. The perception that was voiced as *directions* might possibly indicate an interest in the geometric designing of space. *Balance and weight shift* can point to an attraction towards comprehending the mechanics of physical movement. Noticing an *even pulse* in someone's walk could signify a fascination with rhythm, while *a man looking* could mean someone is more intrigued by character and story than abstract movement. An overall pattern of what we enjoy emerges through the process of doing and watching many improvisations. In this way we clarify what we like doing as performers and what tickles our fancy as an audience member.

To develop the style of performing that is unique to us we need to expand our feedback vocabulary to include in our observations not only what is being done but also the nature of how it is being done. Again I performed 'a man walking' but not in such a neutral way as on the first occasion. I introduced small variations of speed and a shifting of vision, sometimes looking in different directions not just straight ahead. Every once in a while I came to a full stop. I also included minute movements of lips, eyebrows, and cheeks. I asked the students to write down three different things in five words or less, relating to what they saw as I was walking, and three things, also in five words or less, that described how I was doing something. I also posed the question, 'Is there a connection between what they were seeing and how I was doing it?'

A few answers to

'What did you see?'	How something was done
A worried man	*Pinched, eye brows*
Walking without conviction	*Stopping, going, hesitation*
Someone looking for someone	*Clear focus of eyes*
An erratic use of locomotion	*Stopped walking abruptly*
Looking at an imaginary person	*Looking with eyes wide open*

David Wells, a student of mine who has developed a wonderful comic style of performing, is a good subject to use as an example of what someone is doing and perceiving how he does it. What I see as I watch David perform is a humorous character that is always on the go and in constant conflict with forces which surround him. The character is cheeky and mischievous. David creates this character for me through the use of locomotion, the timing of his looking at the audience, and his stick-figure like movement quality. He is a space gobbler who uses long loping strides in a lovely rhythmic connection to whatever music is playing. An undulating, bobbing and weaving of his torso and head adds a light-hearted feeling to his travels through space. The use of his face primarily through the movement of his eyes and lips can elicit a large range of emotion: surprise, concern, determination, delight etc. His vision shifts between looking directly at an imaginary person or object and the audience inviting those of us watching into his world. David's sense of comic timing, his judgement of when and how long to travel through space, when to look at the audience, when to stop and pull a face and then continue on his journey also adds to his style which makes most people in the audience laugh whole-heartedly.

Through detailing how someone creates certain effects – such as assuming certain postures which depict loneliness, eliciting laughter by jumping madly around the room or by modulating one's voice to more readily engage an audience – students will acquire the vocabulary necessary for the development of a strong performance technique. The willingness to look for and define, in their own words, the theatrical elements they find interesting will allow them to create their own exercises to enhance the skills that are important to them.

In the search for clarity, *how?* and *what?* are complementary questions. How are we being entertained? If it is through humour what is the performer doing to create the comedy? In what ways are we being entertained? It is helpful also to ascertain which of the four modes – pedestrian, character, caricature or abstract – a performer is utilising to engage our interest, and to understand whether it is the performer's skill or a theatrical device which is enhancing the performance being watched. Two forms of feedback can be used to answer these questions, the general and the detailed. The former, which is a useful step in the development of the detailed version, tends to rely on surface rather than probing statements, whereas detailed feedback aims to elaborate on how certain effects are being created and how these in turn impact upon whoever is giving the feedback.

Let's examine the distinction by using a hypothetical example relating to an abstract movement piece. Some general feedback might be: *'I loved the articulation of your movements John'*. This is perfectly valid feedback to give someone, and it emphasises at least one element enjoyed by the watcher. A detailed description, however, of the same performance would work in a more precise way. *'I loved the clarity of articulation in your movements John, especially the way you moved between motion and stillness. The beginning section where your legs were still and you did that beautiful in-place dancing just using your arms and torso I found to be very sensual'*.

Here is another example, this time of a performance that combines text and movement. The general feedback: *'Wow, that was inspired, Sally. The character seemed so real even though the story itself was quite surreal and the language very rich. I also loved your singing, you have a beautiful voice. I could listen to it forever'*. The detailed feedback: *'Wow, that was inspired, Sally. Your simple use of gesture and the darting use of vision created for me a strong reality of a frightened woman in a strange environment. I also loved your singing, the gentle soulful use of your lower pitch range and the fact that you chose to sing a sad slow song facing upstage so that we could not see your face made me feel that your character was yearning to return to a previous way of life'*. Clearly, more understanding of our personal aesthetics is gained when detailed feedback is used.

The self-teacher isolates and develops the skills that are necessary to engage an audience. It is paramount that students add to this their inner-director's understanding of how to manifest the emotional and contextual elements of a performance. As I have said previously the improviser must wear many hats and assume responsibility for the entire package being presented to the audience. It is therefore essential for improvisers to blend well-designed stagecraft with performing expertise.

Let's reiterate some of the skills that one develops as a performer. There are the physical ones flexibility, strength, speed, balance, rhythm and coordination, which we generally associate with dancers. Then there are the vocal: enunciation, pitch, control, sound and volume, which are part of the actor's and singer's domain. These are the obvious skills in which actors and dancers must become proficient in order to ply their trade and should be practiced by anyone wishing to be more articulate in their physical and verbal communication. There are also less obvious skills such as the use of vision which creates a sense of conviction in an actor's work and helps to clarify the intention of a dancer's movement. The ability to soften or harden the texture of the body to produce different moods is also a valuable tool for the performer to develop.

Other performing skills that can be observed, remarked upon, and therefore chosen for personal development by a student include:

-- use of posture

-- subtle variations of speed in movement and or speech

-- the use of silence and stillness

-- integration of vision with movement

-- variations in locomotion

Let's include some devices used by directors to create interest and clarity in performances:

-- creating visual interest via the placement of performers on stage

-- the slowing down and speeding up of the action

-- timing of entrances and exits

-- the ebb and flow of emotional tensions

-- the use of costumes, music and lighting to heighten effects

These are only a few of the possible observations students can make regarding a skill or theatrical device. I offer them to the reader as examples of what is possible to observe and name in order to begin developing a vocabulary that will allow you to find a deeper understanding of what you enjoy theatrically. I implore you to look for the insect on the leaf of a branch of a tree in the middle of a forest.

The most important aspect in developing one's use of positive feedback is not just committing to memory what we learn from our teachers or through the reading of books, but to acquire the confidence in our own observations and the ability to create the names and descriptions that allow for the continuing development of ourselves as improvising performers.

9
FINISH YOUR TALK AND LET'S GATHER

The phrase I most often use in my classes is the one above. It signals the end of the cognitive learning sessions during the first half of all my workshops. It's my call to students to finish the feedback discussions with their duet partners that follow the completion of each score. I remember clearly the decision to use this refrain when I first included the partnering section in my classes. It was back in 1984 when I shifted from group oriented scores to duet scores as a predominant structure of the non-performing portion of class. It was the most obvious thing to say and, though I tried to think of other more interesting phrases, none came to mind. Very quickly I began enjoying saying this sentence several times in each class. It has a nice rhythm to it and the words 'let's gather' elicit the sense of a warm communal happening. Several years later, after what seemed like several thousand repetitions of the phrase, a student, Louise Wignal, suggested that 'finish your talk and let's gather' should be the name of a chapter in this book.

I had no idea what the actual subject matter of the chapter would be. Three years later and half way through the writing it dawned on me that it would be the last chapter since *finish your talk and let's gather* implies something is coming to a conclusion, but I still did not have an inkling of what it might contain. Finally, six years after Louise gave me the first name of a chapter and after all the other chapters had been named and completed, I realized what the content would be. *Finish your talk* symbolises the end of my writing. It has been an exercise or score I gave myself, to express in words what I find valuable in the body of knowledge which has evolved from my teaching over the past forty years. This book therefore is a cognitive learning process that I've put myself through and it has proved an important element in furthering my development as a teacher. After many years of demanding of students that they find the words (through positive feedback) to describe why they like doing what they do I finally put my own words on paper to describe what I found so wonderful about improvisation.

And let's gather, the second half of my call to bring students together in preparation for the next score, will hopefully become material for another book, one that I definitely will not write. In response to 'Is there going to be another book after this one?' put to me by a very dear friend and student, Michael Shaw, I immediately replied 'No way!'. We had been walking to a pub to watch the Grand Final footy match between Collingwood and Brisbane and his question took me by surprise. My answer however was something I've known for over a year now. In fact the thought that once I finish this book I will never have to write again has been the impetus for a final burst of writing that is bringing my career as an author to an end I welcome with open arms and relieved fingers. The written word is too permanent for me, too much like a well-rehearsed performance piece where there is too little room for improvisation. Once the words are printed and bound in a book they can never change. But I change constantly and so does my teaching. I've rewritten the *Positive Feedback* chapter three times. The last was completed several weeks ago. This sentence was completed at 8:25am Australian Eastern

Standard time on the 14th of May 2004. Already I want to change elements of my *Eye to Eye - Positive Feedback* chapter. But I won't. This book will never be finished if I try to keep improvising with it.

Words written by people who love to write are beautiful things. They come alive and sing and dance on the page creating a piece of theatre that can be enjoyed by millions of people over thousands of years. This is a magical thing that improvisation can never achieve. So I can very honestly say I love the written word, it's just that I prefer others to do it! A few minutes after I confessed my feelings about writing to Michael I thought of an idea that might be a good follow up to *The Wonder of Improvisation.* I would ask several of my past and present students to gather (metaphorically speaking of course) and present them with this score: *'Do a piece of writing discussing what elements of my teaching influenced you to the extent that you are using them in your own work. It is very important that you discuss how you have changed and evolved what you learnt from me in order to develop yourself as a performer or teacher.'*

I won't have to do any writing and yet the writing will still go on. I would love to read about what another generation of improvisers is doing in their teaching and performing of this art form. I would also like to know how people who are not performers have used some of my teachings in their work and everyday experiences.

So much has already been written about improvisation. Much more will be written in the future. I suggest you also try Ruth Zaporah's *Action Theatre - The Art of Presence,*[10] Steve Nachmonovich's *Free Play – Improvisation in Life and Art,*[11] and 'Contact Quarterly',[12] a magazine put out in the United States.

And now that I have finished my talk it is time for me to go out and play. I've suddenly found an enjoyment and confidence in performing that I have never felt before. For someone involved in the performing arts business for over forty years I've spent very

---

[10] Action Theater   Published by North Atlantic Books Berkeley California 1995
[11] Free Play   Published by Jeremy P. Tarcher Los Angeles California 1990
[12] Editors Nancy Stark Smith, Lisa Nelson. PO Box 603 Northampton Massachusetts

little time in front of an audience, rather I've been behind the scenes, influencing and encouraging others to perform. Teaching has always been my first love. It has engaged the creative aspect of my mind whereas performing requires a more disciplined use of the body, something I really haven't spent enough time on. There is a saying in the performing arts community that has always annoyed me because it puts teachers on a much lower pedestal than performers: 'Those that can, do, those that can't, teach'. Though I admit there might be a smidgen of truth to this claim the teacher in me has added a sequel: 'Those who do can't do without those who can teach'.

So it is with great delight that at the age of sixty-two the performer in me is gathering strength and will be putting into practice what I have been teaching for these many years. But I won't always be doing it alone. Two long-time students and friends, Lindesay Dresdon (on my left) and John Fenelon (on my right), both over sixty years old, will be joining me (the one with the long hair) in the performing trio 'Men of Pause', helping me present to audiences the wonder of improvisation.

APPENDIX

A SCORE OF SCORES

This appendix contains some of the many scores I have used in my classes to help students become more articulate with their physicality, their use of language, the combination of movement and text, and the interrelationship between themselves and the other improvisers in duet and small group work. Some scores I have used several times over the thirty years I have been teaching improvisation, some I have used just once, and there might be one or two that I have yet to use. It is not in my nature to repeat things too often even though reiteration is a valuable learning tool. Rather it's in the nature of my teaching and my personality to experiment continuously with new ideas. I strongly suggest you find your own balance between creative experimentation and development through repetition. It is so important that you be true to yourself and the process that fits your personality.

I offer these scores, listed below, as a guide for teachers who wish to create an improvisation section in their classes, or for those who wish to do their own practice sessions as a means of experimenting with various styles of movement-based extemporaneous theatre. The scores cover some of the basic principles of physical articulation with self, physical articulation with others, interrelationship with an audience, and the development of voice and use of language. Use any that interest you and include some positive feedback, talking about what of value you perceived while doing a score and things you enjoyed when watching others engage with it. Delving into the reasons why you find certain things valuable will help you to develop your own scores and further clarify and enhance a performance style which is truly unique to yourself.

The scores are given in this regular typeface. The value for using these scores has been put in *italics*.

1. *BASIC ARTICULATORS*
2. *THE NECESSARY ARTICULATOR*
3. *SPATIAL RELATIONSHIPS*
4. *VISION*
5. *SOUND SCORES*

Basic articulators (in place, still and locomotion)

These scores are designed to explore movement possibilities in each of the basic articulators. They are usually done with partners so students can gain maximum interactive value. The importance of acknowledging and using the basic articulators as valuable physical vocabulary cannot be overstated. They are as significant as flexibility work in a dance class, or using the words 'yes, no, you, me' in any language.

In place scores: (moving as much as you like so long as you stay in place)

- **Playing in place: variations in size and speed**

Decide which of you will be the initiator, which the responder. Using your hands as the primary mover, explore the effects of varying the size and speed of movement. Repeat this three times, changing the primary mover from hands, to head, to legs, then to torso.

Size and speed of movement is the most obvious way we have of varying and therefore creating interest in our movement patterns. Similarly the use of different primary movers helps to augment diversity within our physicality.

- **Playing in place: special relationships**

Without moving your feet explore opening, closing and maintaining the space between yourself and your partner.

The limitation of keeping the feet on the floor heightens the awareness and enjoyment of smaller movements, and elicits more precise and playful use of timing in order to create sustained interest between participants.

- **Playing in place: moving in planes**

While in close proximity to your partner let most of your movements be in the vertical plane (up and down). Next explore movements that stay primarily in the horizontal plane (movements that are parallel to the floor). As a final exercise while still doing some close in place dancing with a partner at times move in different spatial planes' at times join each other moving in the same plane.

Exploring the interrelationship of vertical and horizontal movements has an interesting side effect. The changing of levels between the dancers lends itself to some very interesting shapes.

- **Playing in place: proximity**

Explore three movement pieces from different spatial relationships with your partner; One in close proximity, one a long distance away (at least seven meters), and one at medium distance (about three meters).

Practicing relating to someone at different distances helps to break the habit of wanting to be in the comfort zone of normal social spacing. Theatrically, the variance of distance helps create distinct dramatic tensions as well as varying the sculptural landscape of a performance.

Locomotion scores: travelling from one place to another

- **Taking a step   a step in three parts**

There are three parts to a step: the moment your foot leaves the floor, when it travels through the air and when it reconnects with the floor. Take the time to emphasise each of these actions making the moment the foot leaves the floor a more important part of the step than the other two, and vice versa.

This score is a wonderful means of getting students to realise how it is possible to play creatively with something as simple as taking a step. It is also a useful way of teaching them to break an action down into parts, the better to explore and improvise with it)

- **Taking a step: size and speed**

Vary the size and speed of your steps. Articulating the transitions (acceleration and deceleration of speed, increasing and decreasing size) as well as the end points, adds just that bit more colour to the performance.

It is always worthwhile to exercise variations of size and speed as a means of altering the physical energy being used to create movement. This in turn varies the emotional dynamics of an improvisation.

- **Taking a step: take one step backwards**

Let's challenge the natural tendency to travel in a forward direction by doing a score that eliminates it. The only way you are allowed to locomote is either backwards, sideways or diagonally.

By eliminating the predominant pattern of forward movement students are forced to discover a new and interesting physical vocabulary. This would be effective in 'in- place' and 'stillness' scores too so have your students explore in-place, still and locomotion movements which have only a sideways, backwards or diagonal orientation.

- **Taking a step: how far do you go**

Pay attention to and play with two things: the distance covered each time you travel, and the actual shape of the pathway you are taking, whether it be circular, straight, zigzag or undefined.

We tend to limit the length of our locomotions by thinking we have to fit them to the dimensions of the space we're working in. Yet we can diversify our notions of longer-length transits, for example by rounding corners or affecting an about-face when approaching a wall.

149

Dancing with stillness: (being absolutely still but still feeling like you're dancing)

- **The power of stillness: enlivening stillness**

One partner is only allowed to do still and locomotion movements while the other is limited to in-place and still moving. Switch roles halfway through.

This score will help develop an awareness of the variety of potential relationships which exist between the basic articulators. Stillness is a movement that can be observed and related to. Do not become a frozen statue. Hold whatever shape you are in with whatever tension you chose to give it. Observe and acknowledge the relationship of people moving in place, locomoting or being still in relationship to your stillness.

- **The power of stillness: duration and timing**

Play with the length of time in stillness. Each partner in turn affects a movement, which takes no longer than a second to complete before they must be still. They must then wait until their partner completes his or her movement before they move again. The interplay is the variation in the length of stillness.

There are two important elements here. One is to play with the length of time you hold your stillness. The other is to feel the duet stillness (both still together) and create erratic and challenging rhythms with each other. This is a game that develops aliveness in stillness because of the necessity to be alert to each other's timing.

- **The power of stillness: a journalistic view of stillness**

This four-part sequence takes about an hour to complete, including feedback between partners after each sequence. Though the emphasis is on stillness it is the dance that happens in-between the still points that helps to determine the where, what, when and how of the stillness.

The essence of these scores is to highlight the act of stillness. Using four of the five journalistic questions "where, when, what and how" helps to magnify the importance and power of stillness when using movement in performance. Asking the student to choose where they begin their stillness initiates a more thoughtful creation of the visual landscape being presented to an audience.

a) Where in the room does your stillness begin?

As performers when we acknowledge that we are a shape in a landscape (the performing space) and that every time we are still we create a living photograph, the choice of where we stop moving becomes important.

b) As well as recognising where stillness begins also play with when the stillness ends.

The question 'when?' in this case allows the student to explore the dramatic impact of the duration of their stillness.

c) What is the shape of your stillness?

Another score that explores the myriad of possible visual images we can create.

d) How does you stillness begin? How does it end?

With this question the student examines the transitional possibilities of approaching and leaving stillness.

2. The necessary articulator (initiating and responding)

Humans are social animals and automatically communicate and negotiate with each other, seeking through the device of initiation and response the most pleasurable or meaningful relationship we can achieve. The following scores are designed to heighten the ability to initiate and respond, to specify, without expectation or control, a means of exchanging information so that the creation of a valuable experience is equally shared. Each score begins with designated initiator and responder role-play. Students stay in their chosen roles until the facilitator tells them to switch. The initiator is not doing a solo. She is putting out physical information (jumping, raising an arm, turning around, etc.) simply to see how the responder responds to the movement.

- **Initiator responder role play: clear and simple**

The initiator always works with her eyes closed. For safety's sake movements should be limited to in place and still dancing. The responder works with all three of the basic articulators – moving towards, away from, around and with the initiator – aiming to create an aesthetically pleasing experience for himself while at the same time responding to the initiator. After several minutes change roles.

Since the initiator cannot see what response is being elicited from the responder the necessity to be simple and clear with movement becomes important. Initiating is not soloing. The intention is to illicit responses from one's partner. Because the initiator cannot see a response he will tend to simplify and be more definite in his movements.

- **Initiator responder role play: travelling with a partner**

The initiator and responder must always travel, be still or do in place movements at the same time as each other. The responder does not necessarily have to copy the initiator. Her movements can be different, travelling can be in different directions and she can be in different shapes while being still. Or they can at times be similar. Explore this one in duets, trios or even larger groups. As students' ability to respond quickly develop you might even try removing the designated initiator role.

A simple score but very valuable as a means of paying attention and responding quickly to changes that occur in an improvisation. The designated initiator must be definite each time they change from one basic articulator to another. The responders have to stay alert and attuned to any possible change. When the initiator role is eliminated the fun really begins as no one knows who is going to effect the change.

3. Spatial relationships

Landscaping, or space shaping, are terms I use to describe the placement of performers in an environment. Where performers stand in a studio in relation to the various walls — and especially to the audience — helps to create a dramatic effect. Being close to the audience, standing with the back facing the audience, crouched in a corner or standing upright in the centre of the room will have an effect on the improvising performer as well. Acknowledging and defining the spatial relationships between performers, whether improvising as part of a duet or in small or large groups, plays an important part in creating visual interest for an audience and stimulates interaction among the participants.

• **Physical space: how close, how far**
Open, close and maintain the space between you and your partner.
I have yet to create a score that can be put more simply, be understood by everyone, and yet which offers so much scope for engaging with a variety of experiences. Students can explore the exercise in a totally abstract way or find and develop situations between characters or caricatures. Reminding them to be clear with their basic articulators helps to specify what is happening in the event. Further useful layers are to have partners spend some time maintaining long, close and medium distances from each other. This will get them to practise and be comfortable developing material from a variety of distances.

• **Physical space: the walls are your partners**
Make, break and maintain physical contact with your partner and or the walls.
It is interesting how little the perimeter of a studio is used unless specified by the teacher. By making students more aware of this option the energy and physicality in a duet becomes much more active. Locomotion will tend to have a greater variety of speeds. The entire space in the studio is filled with more energy as students move from wall to wall, crisscrossing the space. The

addition of physical contact (this is the closest students can be to each other in spatial terms) develops a sense of trust. Making and breaking contact, whether this is with a partner or the wall, is a task that absorbs the creative energy of students. They easily get involved in exploring the various ways they can support and distribute their weight on the inanimate, unmoveable object of the wall and the more pliable moveable body of their partners.

4. Vision

      I think of vision as the fifth appendage, as important as one's arms and legs in the use of communicating through physical movement. During the personal physical play section of my class I always direct students to be aware of what they are looking at, and that there are three basic foci that vision naturally shifts between: the body, the environment, and the people within the environment. Being clear about what you are actually seeing is one of the best ways I know of bringing yourself into the present and allows for actions and reactions to occur in a more spontaneous manner.

- **The fifth appendage: drawing lines**

Look directly at the fingertips of one hand while slowly moving it through space. Gradually move the hand faster and faster, making sure your vision doesn't fall behind or move ahead of the fingertips. Find ways of shifting your vision from the fingertips of one hand to the other without losing sight of the pathway created by the moving fingers. Challenge yourself by changing levels, speed, and size of movements.

      This might sound easy but it really requires a lot of concentration to keep your vision constantly and precisely on your fingertips. This exercise is designed to create a direct connection between vision and body movement. It will also help to develop a more coordinated movement connection between arms, head and torso.

- **The fifth appendage: who are you looking at**

Look towards, away from, and with your partner. This can be done in duet or trio form and encourages students to practise the timing of when to look at and when to look away from their partners, as well as to explore the communication value of looking at the same thing with a partner.

This is a great way of instilling a sense of story into abstract movement. The implication of acceptance and rejection will invariably occur in a quite humorous fashion.

- **The firth appendage: three ways of looking**

There are three ways of observing a partner: direct looking, peripheral looking and unsighted looking. Explore what happens movement-wise when the use of vision shifts between these three. Direct looking does not necessarily mean eye to eye contact; you can be looking, for example, directly at your partner's foot. Peripheral looking signifies that all information is being received out of the corner of your eye. In unsighted looking your partner is somewhere behind you but you are still trying to look at him or her as if you had eyes in the back of your skull.

Whatever the reason, most dancers have developed a habit of taking in information primarily through peripheral vision. This score helps to expand visual patterns of behaviour by including the more humanistic direct looking and the highly unusual unsighted looking as well as the peripheral perception of a partner. By looking at partners in these different ways a strong sense of connection is established and the ability to send and receive information is increased.

5. Sound scores

Vocal sounding is a very strong personal power source for me. With it I can express a wide range of emotional moods, which in turn enhance communication of my postures, gestures and abstract movements. I can also elicit a lot of laughter through the

I added a balance and turning routine to the swaying. By the simple act of lifting a knee while swaying, varying degrees of turns were accomplished, depending on the initial force of the sway. The hard thing was to keep the knee lift simple and straight in front of the body, not really thinking about the turn but letting it happen purely as a result of the swinging arms.

After several minutes of this gentle swaying and turning I had the participants just hang over their legs with their knees bent slightly so their fingertips touched the floor. We stayed in this position for a minute or two just relaxing and feeling the natural loose hanging weight of our head, torso and arms. Compared with women most men have tighter hamstrings. I found that trying to stretch my hamstrings while sitting on the floor and reaching out over straight legs tended to tighten my lower back muscles. The *Hang Over* sequence was designed to let gravity do the work while the only muscular activity I did was to gently straighten and bend my knees. Again the most difficult thing was to keep it simple. The object is to let the body hang over the legs, avoiding the desire to push muscularly closer to the ground. As knees are straightened the weight of the torso, arms and head will elongate the hamstrings. I don't try to keep my fingertips on the floor but let them ride up and down according to the level of my flexibility of the moment.

By varying the positions of feet and torso in the *Hang Over* pose the elongation process effects various muscle groups in the upper leg. A welcomed and unanticipated offshoot of this exercise was that, through gentle repetition, it also strengthened the quadriceps.

This brought us to the *Ups and Downs*. Using various body parts (head, hip, arm, hand, foot, etc.) as a primary source of movement, I had participants lift and lower themselves towards and away from the floor. The degree of lift was varied, sometimes going fully to standing, sometimes moving just a few centimetres up and down. Weight could be taken on the feet or the back, hands and feet combined, knees, shoulders or whatever body parts the student chose to use for support. This was the strengthening section of my workout. It also allowed bodies to become comfortable and creative with movements into and out of the floor.

In this score, which I sometimes call 'sound mirrors', I have students sit and face each other and look intently at each other's mouths. In each pair one is the leader, the other the follower. The leader clearly and slowly starts making sounds. The follower attempts to duplicate the sound at exactly the same time as the leader is making it. When the leader feels that the follower is mirroring correctly he or she can gradually become more challenging with the sound making.

The child-like game aspect of this score has a very freeing effect on students' sound making. The fun of seeing our faces being mirrored, as well as the sound, instils a playfulness to the explorations of our noises which otherwise might be lacking. A variation to this score is to do the same exercise but to use words. The leader starts speaking slowly, making sure it is easy for the follower to say the same thing at the same time. The leader gradually increases the verbal speed, seeing how close the pair can get to normal speaking without the follower getting lost.

6. Verbal starters

Verbal starters are a good name for these scores as the intention is to prevent the editor inside us from stifling our use of words in the performing space, and for students to begin a search for what I call their own theatrical language. Theatrical language is the style of speaking which the student feels most comfortable using when performing an improvised monologue in front of an audience. Styles can range from normal pedestrian speech to poetic prose to abstract fractured sentences.

- **Verbal starter: constant talking**

Two minutes of constant talking. With stop watch in hand I have students work in pairs. They sit facing each other, taking it in turn to deliver a two-minute monologue while the other listens. Their brief is to talk slightly faster than normal, never stopping the flow of words. It can be total nonsense, a word can be repeated several times, and there might be logical sections and illogical sections. Content should not be a concern but use of sounds is not allowed.

Don't think! Talk! This is the essence of this score and it generally elicits a lot of laughter from the person listening. Quite often an interesting turn of phrase will emerge from this score. A short feedback session allowing both listener and talker to recall what phrases or juxtaposition of images they enjoyed helps to build students' confidence in being extemporaneous speakers.

- **Verbal starter: one word sentences**

This score is the flip side of constant talking. Students again work in pairs, performing talking solos to each other. This time however they can only talk in one-word sentences. It is the way a word is spoken and the timing of the silences between words which enables each word to assume the importance of a full sentence.

In this exercise the content or meaning of the spoken word is conveyed through the body language and emotional timbre of the voice. After each student has had a turn I have him or her repeat the score a few times and become aware of how the silence between words is just as important as the words themselves. This allows students to perform the thinking/feeling process which is a natural part of normal speech.

7. Words and movement

Too often movement takes a back seat when a student first begins adding improvised text to their performances. While this works well for those who seem to find a strong creative source through the use of the spoken word, a large majority of students actually use movement as a stimulus for finding the images, thoughts or feelings that they wish to express through words. I therefore keep looking for ways to combine physical language with verbal language. As I do with all my teaching I have students explore many ways of mixing these two types of communication until they ultimately evolve what suits them best.

- **Body, voice and words: moving – talking – looking**

The following exercise uses the constant-talking score as a base and adds the interplay of the basic articulators (in place, still and locomotion) as a physical adjunct. With one partner sitting and listening the other does two minutes of constant talking shifting between the basic articulators as she does so. Partners then switch roles. After both have had a turn and have given some positive feedback about what was enjoyable both as talkers and listeners I have them repeat the exercise. This time the speaker is to clarify, through use of vision, who is being spoken to: the self, the partner, an imaginary person, or the universe.

Students will naturally approach this movement score in a variety of ways. Some will be quite abstract in their movements while others will use gestures and postures more indicative of someone speaking. The more students practise variations of this score the clearer they become about how they would like to blend abstract and gesture with speech. Voice texture also becomes more dynamic as movement becomes more dynamic and, interestingly, the movement in many cases helps the flow of words by stimulating images for students to talk to or about. You can take this score a step further and have the two students enact the talking simultaneously.

- **Body, voice and words: talking in gibberish**

Have each student do a monologue for the whole class using only gibberish. Make sure that there is a balanced use of consonant and vowel sounds.   After everyone has had a turn, discuss what theatrical elements the students found valuable both as doers and audience. Now set them working in pairs and dialoguing with each other in gibberish.

Monologues and dialogues using gibberish, or gobbledegook as some people call it, are very simple scores and a good initial step to help students use the speaking voice. The gibberish, if spoken with a good balance of consonant and vowel sounds, does sound like a language. It frees students of the concern to produce 'interesting' verbal content since actual words are not being used.

159

- **Body, voice words: gibberish to English**

A more advanced play with gobbledegook can be done in either duet or trio form. Begin with all participants having a conversation in gibberish that has some variation of emotions. (This usually happens quite naturally.) A couple of minutes into the conversation call out the name of one of the performing students. This student must now talk in legible speech; the others maintain talking in gibberish. A couple of minutes later have the other student begin talking legibly. Eventually all performers should be speaking in their real language. Whoever speaks first should not say anything to the effect of, "Sorry I can't understand a word you're saying" as this would undermine the object of the exercise which is to create an interesting dialogue between two or three people.

Talking in gibberish quite naturally gets people to put more expression into their voice and body language. The emotional interaction becomes established in the first two minutes so that when the first of the real language is spoken it simply adds factual information to the emotional story line. I have found this score to be very good at helping students develop skills at improvising with conversational material.

- **Body, voice and words: Gilbert and Sullivan**

You can take the score one step further by using the Gilbert and Sullivan mode.   Instead of them speaking in gibberish have students sing and relate to each other in the manner of light opera.

This ups the humour quotient of the emerging story both in the use of physical and verbal language. Humour is a wonderful tool for developing confidence in the improvising performer. As their confidence grows students will more easily adapt to creating more serious language as part of their performance.

- **Body, voice and words: from gibberish to ghost stories.**

This score is done with the whole class sitting in a circle as if they are at a campfire on a dark night telling scary stories. A ghost story is told with each student taking fifteen seconds to a minute to add their bit to the progressing story then passing it on to the person on their right.   They are instructed to use exaggerated gestures and postures and to address the story to various individuals around the circle, to themselves, the universe or an imaginary being outside the circle. Initially all the story telling is done in well-enunciated gibberish. As the story passes around the circle a second time the storyteller starts talking in gibberish but switches to well-enunciated English words half way through. Each succeeding speaker repeats the pattern.

The object here is to have students pay a lot of attention to the physicality of gesturing, posturing, looking and enunciating, Students will find that the actual words of the story will flow more easily. The movements of the body and the sound of the speaking actually help to generate a vibrant use of language.

8. Small group scores

I inevitably end the first half of my classes with a small group (three to five people) or large group (six or more) score as a means of getting students to expand their awareness of the bigger picture. Duets help build skills in negotiating what form an improvisation will take, in sharing in the development of material and in maintaining a consistent flow from beginning to end. In group work however it becomes exponentially more difficult to find coherence in an improvisation with each additional person that is added to the mix. Finding agreement becomes more challenging as the necessity for simplifying the visual information being presented becomes paramount otherwise chaos will be the only thing being created. The larger the group the more students must give up their own individual creative ideas and respond with similarity to someone else's impulse. If everyone in a group is merely responding in a similar way to everyone else however a boring inertia sets in. Hence students must be aware of the total picture being presented and blend themselves into that picture whilst also being willing to initiate changes and help shift the energy of the emerging improvisation.

- **Group awareness   who is following whom**

Explore the necessary articulator (initiating and responding) within small groups. Form trios and have students work in a two to one situation. Initially have one person in each group take the role of initiator with the remaining two as responders. Then switch roles so that the two responders are the initiators and the original initiator is the sole responder. You can also play with this shifting of roles by designating one duet within the quartet to initiate and the other to respond. Switch roles after several minutes.

There is a hidden agenda here. Both the initiating and responding duets must find agreement on what to initiate and how to respond. There are no designated roles between the partners within each duet. Their agreement about what to do is silently worked out by the doing itself.

- **Group awareness: similarity by the numbers**

This score is designed to have students practice similarity within all the possible numerical interrelationships in a group. Within a trio the possibilities are three together, two to one and three separate. The task is to have moments during the improv when all three are doing the same thing, times when two are doing so and times when everyone is doing something different. In a quartet I designate the possibilities as four together, four apart, three to one, two to two or two to one to one. I have created an acronym ROMP (Relationship Of Mathematical Possibilities) as a light hearted semantic key that helps to foster cohesion within group improvisations.

Altering the relationships numerically helps make students aware of the interactions of smaller groups within the larger community. These interactions can be totally abstract and deal solely with the spatial relationships of individuals within each of the sub-groups as well as the spatial relationship between the sub-groups. Or they can take on a more theatrical element of a power struggle between two groups.

- **Group awareness: the primary mover**

This is a good score for quartets and quintets. Have all members in the group stay within the same basic articulator as each other. They all must travel together or do in-place dancing together or be absolutely still together. They do not however have to do the same movements.

By designating a base of similarity, in this case the basic articulators, the element of everyone doing one thing together while also doing something different is explored. I initially have each person in the group take turns being the initiator and then dispense with the initiating role. This develops a heightened attentiveness to the activities of everyone in the group as well as enhancing the ability to react quickly to changes within a shifting group setting.

9. Large group scores

The most important element in devising group scores is to find ways to simplify the visual information that is presented to the audience.   The Melbourne performance troupe 'Born in a Taxi' originally performed their improvisations in a large group format sometimes using as many as twelve people.   They had a very simple structure called 'school of fish'.   The whole group would stand facing in the same direction and whoever was in front would be the leader.   Everyone would do the same thing as the leader. This created a single visual event for the audience.   Whenever the leader rotated left or right the facing of the group changed, automatically putting someone else in the leadership role. The additional element of having a solitary figure that remained outside the group (doing whatever he wanted to do) created very humorous symbolic representations of the individual versus the mob, the outcast versus the in-group.   Even when *Taxi* changed from a large group to a small group of five people they still continued to use "school of fish" in their practice.   Over several years they have become very adept at unison movement and adjusting to sudden shifts of theatrical development offered by any of the group of five.

Their improvised performances look like well-rehearsed choreography yet have that wonderful sense of immediacy and excitement inherent in improvisation.

- **Keep it simple: lines, dots and clumps**

This is a very simple score that helps sculpt the performance space while allowing for a large range of individuality of movement within the group. I call it 'Lines, Dots and Clumps'. The score consists of students creating lines or clumps with other students or isolating themselves as a dot in space. They can change their orientation at any time but should always be aware of the overall picture being created by the group. An interesting addition to the score is to have the lines and clumps recognize and play with their clarity of in-place, still and locomotion togetherness.

I have used this with as many as twenty students. It helps to create a clear visual landscape, a kaleidoscopic image of lines and clumps getting larger and smaller with individuals emerging from groups doing their thing then being reassimilated into a group)

- **Keep it simple: the collective unconscious**

I call these 'The Collective Unconscious Scores' because of the nature by which information is passed through the group. They are best done in a large group of eight or more people. The basic principle is that each person is responsible for relating with only one or two other people in the group. Here is one of the simplest forms of these scores as an example. Before the improvisation begins each person chooses, in their own mind, one person in the group they plan to respond to. Whenever they look at that person they are to copy the movement of that person. Whenever they are not looking at that person they can move in any way they choose.

I thoroughly enjoy watching the evolution of the group relationship move from chaotic to cohesive. It usually takes two to three minutes for students to recognise and develop the patterns of increasing and decreasing numbers of people doing the same thing. Quite often smiles emerge on students' faces as they realise the interconnections that are happening within the whole group. These scores tend to foster more playful and energetic physicality when someone who wants to do their own thing suddenly sees their movement being mirrored by several people and taking up the challenge tries a few different ways to shake off the copycats.

10. Scores on a theme

Quite often a concept that I begin playing with in the physical play section (warm-up) of my class extends into the partnering section and I end up presenting several scores on a similar theme. This allows for a deeper understanding of the theatrical value of the concept in question. Here is an example of such a class that proved very exciting to me and to the students.

a)   Begin with the spine as primary mover, rounding, twisting and extending. While playing with the spine also include some very small subtle movements of lips and tongue.

(The intent here is to bring an awareness of the face as an active participant in one's movements. It is important that the facial movements stay very subtle and respond to the primary mover in order to make sure the face participates in rather than initiates movement because the tendency is to become grotesque in the use of the face and to let it take over as primary mover.)

b)   Shift the primary mover from spine to arms and hands, bending, straightening and rotating various joints while adding eyebrows to the small movements of lips and tongue.

(I have added another part of the face for students to become aware of. I repeat that the movements of the face should be almost imperceptible. I am trying to enliven the face yet keep a sense of naturalness while doing some personal physical play.)

c)   Shift the primary mover to the legs and add small, subtle movements of the nostrils and cheeks to tongue lips and eyebrows.

(Students really need to hold back now from overusing the face, using it only to respond to the primary mover.)

165

d)   We now move from personal physical play into the partnering section of class. Working in a trio maintain a small and subtle use of the face while doing some subtle and not so subtle movements with the rest of the body. Be precise in the use of basic articulators (in-place, stillness and locomotion).

(For the past year up to the time of this writing I have been talking to students about the possibility of combining abstract movement with their pedestrian persona. I enjoy seeing the person within the dancer, seeing a face that is alive and communicating subtle shifts of emotion as movements speed up, slow down, get larger and smaller. I enjoy seeing dancers look directly at each other possibly sharing a genuine smile. So far this is what these scores have been about, practising putting a human face on a dancer's body.)

e)   Change partners. Now add an exaggerated as well as subtle use of the face along with the subtle and not so subtle movements of the body. Also add designated initiator and responder role-play.

(Here I want students to play with and experience changes of energy and dynamics which come from mixing subtle and not so subtle movements between the face and the body. What emerges when working with the face and body in different degrees of subtlety? What emerges when they work with similar ones?)

f)   Find new partners. The score remains the same with the addition of the initiator now constantly talking until there is a change of roles. After each student has had a turn at initiating finish up with everyone talking at once. When students are doing the constant talking it must always be directed to one or both partners never to the universe, the self or the audience.

(Specifically I want movement to take precedence over the use of language. This is why I used the fast talking format which helps to get rid of the self-editor. It will naturally result in some sensible as well as nonsensical statements being made. Emphasise the clarity of the basic articulators, use of subtle as well as not so subtle use of face and body and the speaking directly to either one

or both partners.   By only directing the talking to a partner students are forced to reorient their bodies as they shift their verbal communication from one partner to the other. This also encourages students to realise that they do not always have to talk to the audience).